Common Sense, Nonsense, or Church Sense

Common Sense, Nonsense, or Church Sense

Hilarious, Hard-hitting Stories Full of God's Truth

Ron Carlson

COVENANT
PUBLISHING

International Standard Book Number 1-892435-07-1

Table of Contents

Preface

hile enjoying the Fourth of July holiday in Seattle several summers ago, I awoke early Sunday morning and strolled down to one of the local coffee houses for a tall latte and a huckleberry scone—the true breakfast of champions. Considering it was only a few minutes past six, I was surprised to find the place nearly full. Folks of various ages and experiences mingled about in their Sunday best—hooded sweatshirts and waffle stompers. Light jazz oozed from the speakers and the smell of fresh ground java tingled my senses. Lethargic souls in search of a jump start had come to the watering hole for a morning jolt. It is a ritual as old as man himself, only the watering holes have changed.

I secured a small table wedged in among some larger ones and sat down to enjoy my brew and the morning *Times*. Surrounding me were tables of six, mostly occupied by younger folks with untamed hair and pierced body parts. Nursing triple-whammy caffeine specials, they were rubbing their eyes and preparing for the big day ahead. Everywhere around me, mini-groups were plotting a course of extreme action. They took turns politicking for their favorite activity.

"Let's go up to Mt. Rainier and play on the glaciers," one suggested.

"No, no, no," said another, "let's go to Mt. Stevens and see the tulip gardens."

"I want to go for a ride on the big ferry up to Victoria," chirped one of the girls. "I hear the whales are playing in the Sound."

"Let's stay here, buy a case of beer, and go to the beach," offered her pragmatic friend.

"Hey, I got my dad's boat," boasted a young man off to my left. "Let's go out to Lake Washington and try our hand at sailing."

"It's my turn to choose," said a disgruntled and obviously neglected bench warmer, "and I want to go bicycling in the Cascades."

"Too much work," his buddy said. "I agree with the beach, babes, and beer idea."

"How about hang gliding on Bainbridge Island?"

"What about antique shopping out in Snohomish?"

"I want to go golfing."

"I want to go to the Space Needle."

"I want to go to the Ballard Locks."

"I want to go bungie jumping."

"I want to go shopping."

"I want to go nuts."

"I want another cup of coffee."

And so it went for an hour or more as these energetic outdoor enthusiasts debated how to spend their precious Sunday. So many options; so little time.

I left the coffee house wide awake but brokenhearted. Of all the options discussed, none mentioned the possibility of attending the church of their choice. None of them advocated an early morning hike to the Divine waterhole. There wasn't a lick of church sense among them. For them, and for a hundred million Americans like them, church is not a viable option. By their way of thinking, church does not make sense. Sunday is a big deal, but church isn't part of it. It is their day, not the Lord's.

A stiff jolt of reality is always stronger than espresso. The events of the morning reminded me that most folks wake up Sunday morning not sure how to spend the day. Work? Play?

Travel? Ski? Shop? Exercise? Rest? Shave? Mow? Shovel? Fish? Scrounge? Hang out? Anything but church.

So who are the weird ones, them or us? Who is wired correctly?

Depends who you ask.

We church people can't imagine what it is like to roll out of bed on Sunday morning and not get ready for church. Unchurched folks can't see the value in wasting a perfectly good day hanging out with self-righteous hypocrites from the planet Straight. Our camp believes church is the most important event of the week. The other camp thinks nearly anything is more important than church. To them it is irrelevant. In our mind they are irreverent. So there you have it: the irrelevant vs. the irreverent.

Church doesn't make sense.

Church is the essence of sense.

Which is it?

I wrote this book because I believe church matters. I think church sense is better than common sense, horse sense, techno-sense, or any sixth sense. My purpose is to encourage and support disciples of the one, true, living God who are seeking identity, meaning, purpose, and salvation in the church of Jesus Christ. It doesn't get any more relevant than this! I am convinced that the most blessed people on this tipsy third rock from the sun are those who "seek first the kingdom and His righteousness" (Matthew 6:33, NKJV). We need an occasional reminder of our true status. Who we are and Whose we are make a huge difference in how we do life.

But I know it ain't easy being a modern day Kingdomite. There are pressures. There are trials. There are temptations. There are hassles. There are issues. There are options. There are Moabites, Midianites, Amorites, and Pleasurites. And some of them bite!

This book makes no claim to be a cure-all for what ails you or the church. It is neither a laundry list of church troubles nor a wish list of sinless solutions. It does offer reinforcement for those who seek to do life on God's terms. It is written primarily for those who subscribe to the idea that spiritual quality of life is superior to temporal quantity and that the "good life" can only be unearthed by reprioritizing earthly attachments. I see the church as the great counterculture movement, subversive and relentless. It is not a human institution, but rather God's spiritual body operating outside conventional wisdom and practice. **It is the ultimate alternative lifestyle.** In some fashion, this is a handbook promoting mutiny "against the rulers, against the powers, against the world forces of this darkness" (Ephesians 6:12).

Because the church movement aligns itself (at least it had better!) in an antagonist posture against the world, we maintain a constant need to understand the human experience through biblical lenses. To progress upward and onward toward spiritual maturity, we require a steady diet of scriptural guidance. There is no shortcut to transformation. My prayer is that this book will help you think church first.

There are many cultural critics better equipped than I to evaluate the tensions existing between the church and the world, and thus I have purposefully chosen not to compete for their turf. I have taken a different perspective. I offer the reader a measure of pagan relief through the ancient but effective means of comic relief. Kingdom business is too serious to take all the Kingdomites seriously!

I suggest that the church has a tendency to be bashful, sometimes too shy to be effective. I advocate a more proactive agenda. I say we take it to the world! Instead of whining about all the abuse we receive, I have concluded a more aggressive style is in the Lord's best interest. We have the best thing going. Why not promote it?

The church would steamroll the world if we could get our act together. Much of what is contained in the following essays tackles the timeless problem of how Kingdomites can stop being their own worst enemies. Call it an internal review, an auditing process of Christian mission and ministry. Fixing ourselves is a prerequisite to fixing the world. Before we can clean up the toxic waste dump, we have to take time to sweep our own porch. To become serious players on the world stage, we had better make sure we "are strong in the Lord, and in the strength of His might" and that we are dressed securely in "the full armor of God" (Ephesians 6:10, 11).

The great battle of the 21st century will not be fought on the plains of Megiddo or in distant space, but between the ears of Earth's six billion plus inhabitants. It will be a war of ideas, philosophies, worldviews, religions, and tidbits. Who prevails will be largely determined by the church's readiness. That means you and me, fellow Kingdomite!

I hope you learn a little, laugh a little, and love a little more.

RON CARLSON

No Car:
No Service

ccompanying eighteen 18-year-old boys/men on a week long trip out of town is an experience for the ages. It becomes doubly interesting when your group stays at a hotel with several hundred other 18-year-old baseball players. It might be best characterized as a testosterone convention.

But it is never boring.

Boys on the road have simple needs: like food and ESPN.

On the third night of the tournament, we played an evening game under the lights that finished about 10 p.m. We got back to the hotel and of course the players were starved. They hadn't eaten for nearly four hours, an unusually long spell between meals.

Next door to the hotel was a strategically placed Burger King® that was making somewhere in the neighborhood of a million dollars a day. Too famished to shower or change clothes, a half-dozen boys, including my always hungry son, made a beeline for Burger King so they could get back in time for Sportscenter.

They came up empty. For security purposes the inside dining area (a benevolent term used in place of "feedlot") closed at 10 p.m.. The only access to burgers and fries was through the drive-in window.

Starving teenagers can be a resourceful lot.

The six of them ran around to the back of the building and huddled in front of the "To Go" menu.

A voice came over the speaker, "I'm sorry, you have to be in a car to order from the drive-through."

The response was wholesale objection. They begged and pleaded for understanding. Their peer inside, invested with authority from the assistant night manager, wouldn't budge. No car: no service.

Refusing to be denied, our boys improvised. They created the illusion of a minivan. You would have had to see it to really appreciate the effort. They had a driver, a front seat passenger, three large boys in the middle seat, all with seatbelts, and a straggler crumpled into the rear cargo area gasping for air.

They eased their imaginary minivan up to the speaker. The driver rolled down the window and pushed the service button.

"May I help you?" the customer-friendly voice inquired.

"Turn down the radio!" a voice shouted from the rear seat, "I can't hear him!"

"Yes," my son responded, as he leaned out the window. "We would like six double-meat cheeseburgers with fries and cokes, no tomatoes or onions, and extra ketchup."

There was an extended pause. A bewildered young face looked out the service window.

"You don't have a car."

"Yes we do," my son argued. "It's a brand new Pontiac minivan, red with chrome wheels!"

"Then why can't I see it?"

"Perhaps because it's late and you're tired," the passenger riding shot-gun suggested.

"You don't have a car and I told you already we can't serve you."

"Trust us; we got a car," my boy pleaded. "Just listen to the awesome stereo!"

With that the six boys broke out in a loud rendition of something from an old Garth Brooks CD. The employee wasn't impressed.

"It's no use," came another voice from the back, "He's blind."

In perfect unison they eased the minivan down the drive, paused at the service window, and laid on the horn. I have never heard such a racket. They waved at the employees gathered there and sped off into the night in their pretend rental van.

It was simply too funny.

Pretending can be wonderful sport, especially late at night with imaginative children in a foreign place. Pretending helps us cope with the drama of life. For the most part it is a harmless exercise that stretches our imaginations and brings some order to the daily grind.

Sometimes, however, pretending can go too far. Like when we play church.

It's a senseless thing to play church. Pretending to be an obedient disciple who loves the Lord, His righteousness, and the narrow way, when in fact, one is prone to do evil and follow the devil's lead is a dangerous prescription for trouble. Genuine faith and obedience cannot be successfully feigned. Discipleship is never make-believe.

Take a moment to examine yourself. Are you the real deal or the great pretender? Does your minivan have wheels? Is your faith journey a child's game or a consuming passion of the heart? Remember, you can't hoodwink God any more than you can the employee of the month at Burger King. He sees right through your silly little scam. Don't waste your time trying to fool God. You'll only make a fool of yourself.

Mouse 101

recent national survey[1] has indicated that calico[2] kittens are the cutest creatures on earth. Even cat-haters[3] have a soft spot in their hearts for these little bundles of fur.

Following the national trend, my blessed mother, experiencing something between a second childhood and acute brain failure after retirement,[4] was recently persuaded

---

[1] I personally conducted the survey. It included my two sisters, my two brothers-in-law, my mother, my two nephews, my niece, my wife, and my unsuspecting neighbor. Though there may be some room for error, it is certainly more accurate than similar polls conducted during the Clinton-Lewinsky affair.

[2] Calico refers to felines of three colors or more, almost always female, and usually of suspect lineage.

[3] A genre of humans who, for many good reasons, refuse to share planet Earth with cats. They have been known to take them swimming on Friday afternoons (while the kids are in school).

[4] This has proven to be a very dangerous stage in the human life cycle. People with too much time on their hands are easily manipulated by the foolish plans of grandchildren. Social scientists call them "suckers."

by her second-grade granddaughter to sponsor a litter of kittens. A few months after the plan was hatched, mama cat hatched a batch of calico cats.

The primary objective for a person with five kittens in the garage is usually to find five weak-minded neighbors who are willing to share the burden.[5] Normally this exchange occurs about six weeks after birth. At nine weeks, my mother still had all five kittens under her sheltering care. "They are too immature to leave their mother," she told me. "They are not even weaned yet."[6]

I tried to reason with the woman, but it was to no avail.[7] "How can you turn a cat out on the street[8] without first attending 'Mouse 101'?" she asked me.

"What exactly is 'Mouse 101'?" I inquired.

"It is the process by which cats learn to catch mice," she patiently explained, "and if kittens aren't provided proper instruction from their mother, they will grow up neurotic."

"Well, we wouldn't want that, now would we?"

"Certainly not!" she exclaimed.

I fell into the trap.[9] For the next fifteen minutes she provided me more details than necessary about the exciting dynamics of "Mouse 101." I'll share just the highlights.

When the kittens turn about six weeks old, mama cat catches an unsuspecting mouse and returns it to the lair.[10] After a brief ritualistic display highlighting her hunting prowess, she eats the mouse. The kittens are impressed. She duplicates the feat the next

---

[5] This act of mercy proves America is a Christian country. Why else would reasonable people act so foolishly?

[6] It has been proven that the best way to wean a kitten is to give it to a neighbor. They learn to eat from a dish in less than thirty minutes.

[7] I think she is still angry at me for leaving the nest before my thirtieth birthday.

[8] Alley is more appropriate than street, but my mother finds the connotations too negative. Instead, she practices positive reinforcement with the kittens: "You were born to be an Aristocat!"

[9] Actually, the cat got my tongue.

[10] In this case, the lair is a custom-made cathouse with electricity, indoor plumbing, and a waterbed.

day, and after a week or so she has the kittens' attention. Her next step is to bring home a live mouse. She then teaches her little ones how to torment their prey. Pretend to let the mouse get away, and then pounce on it. Repeat this act until the mouse goes into coronary shock.[11] Eat the mouse. Head first. Lick your chops. Yum!

The teaching program gets serious when mama cat takes the young'uns, full of bravado and predatory spunk, on a field trip. There she demonstrates the cunning and skill inherent to the species. The kids think she is a cool cat. Instinctively they catch on in a hurry, and for a kitten, catching on means catching lunch.[12]

From the very beginning, "Mouse 101" has a goal: equip the students with the knowledge and skills necessary to become productive and responsible members of the community. This teaching process takes time, patience, and nurturing love.[13]

Following mom's discourse on the merits of "Mouse 101," I realized how important it is for the older to teach the younger, for the mature to equip the immature, and for the experienced to train the inexperienced.

Patterns in nature often serve as valuable lessons on how business should be conducted. We can learn from the ant and the grasshopper, the tortoise and the hare, the cat and the mouse.

While the names of the course headings change depending on the species, the principles and goals are similar: to pass along knowledge and skills in a fashion that equips the young to become productive and responsible members of the community.

Young felines need "Mouse 101." College freshmen need "English 101." Fresh recruits need "Basic Training 101." Rookie pitchers need "Strike Zone 101." New Christians need "Church 101."

---

[11]Cat scientists tell us there is method to the madness. Cats are clean creatures, and they hate to eat dirty prey, so they frighten the mouse repeatedly until the intestines are clear.

[12]Catching lunch is followed by catching a nap. Sleeping is the essence of a cat's existence.

[13]It also helps if the local canine population is chained to their respective porches. A cat's worst nightmare are the words, "This dog can hunt."

A quick review of the New Testament Church Sense Manual confirms the central importance of "Church 101."[14] We must cultivate a church environment characterized by patience, involvement, and nurturing love—an inviting and safe place—a hothouse for spiritual growth. Just as a cat must learn to hunt to survive,[15] so baby Christians must learn to battle sin, grow in the grace and knowledge of Jesus, utilize their spiritual gifts, and reproduce themselves in Jesus.[16] Mature Christians are mandated by the Lord to care for the young'uns. God doesn't give us full-blown, full-bloomed disciples. He brings us babes in Christ and trusts us to raise them in His nurture and admonition.

Brethren, be kind and patient with the young. Position them for spiritual success. Take time to teach them the truth. Pick them up when they fall, dust them off, and get them back on the journey. Above all, love them with the love of the Lord.[17] They are the cutest creatures in the kingdom.

---

[14]For a sampling of this doctrine, read the two volumes of Thessalonians, the Pastoral Epistles, and the Book of Acts. Note the emphasis on "discipling."

[15]This is true in theory, but not at my mother's house. Domestic cats have it made in the shade and are not opposed to flaunting their success.

[16]See the Duncanville Church of Christ's mission statement: *A Spirit-led family seeking to know God, grow in faith, serve others, and share Jesus Christ.*

[17]Roses are red,
Violets are blue,
The mighty oak,
Was once a nut like you.

No Ordinary Place

The place seemed ordinary enough, the tempo nothing special. Regular-looking folks in jeans and sandals tramped along the busy sidewalks like they had somewhere to go. It looked like business as usual. Merchants stood in front of their humble stores hawking imported wares like the week before. Palm trees and flowering bushes separated the concrete jungle from finely manicured lawns.

There were some black Mercedes and some red Jaguars, but most sedans were blue and white and common. Hair was blonder, most of it bleached, but not much bigger. I wasn't overwhelmed with cool.

At a stoplight on west Sunset Blvd., I glanced to the north and there between two plain apartment buildings I saw the sign. Awkwardly resting on a steep hillside about 500 feet above the traffic, the famous white letters spelled the address: H-O-L-L-Y-W-O-O-D.

I don't know what I expected, but something more. Like real big hair, and real big cars, and real big stars. Perhaps a smog-free zone, or a tinsel factory, or free sunglasses with a visit. But not so. Instead it looked like Toronto or Minneapolis or Los Angeles. I didn't feel the magic.

Legends seldom match the hype.

Driving back out of the city on Interstate 10, I realized that Hollywood is more of an attitude than a place. It presents a unique combination of fantasy and reality. It is not only where boy meets girl, but where imagination meets materiality. Hollywood is America's life source.

Hollywood, the attitude, is the most dominant social force in contemporary culture. Hollywood not only shapes how we think and eat and sleep and love, but how we view ourselves and our world. Hollywood interprets both fantasy and reality. It tells us who we are, whose we are, and the hoops we have to jump through to be cool. Hollywood narrates the story of life.

I learned that Hollywood is not a place defined by a boulevard, a strip, or a hotel. Hollywood defies definition. Instead it creates definition. Hollywood owns us: lock, stock, barrel, mind, and soul. We are putty in their hands.

Analyzing and unraveling the Hollywood notion is like squeezing mercury between your fingers—it is everywhere and nowhere. It is by accident and on purpose. Harmless and fun on some fronts, ugly and destructive on others, it represents mankind at their creative best and their depraved worst. Hollywood manifests the Seven Deadly Sins in abundance while simultaneously promoting animal rights. The silver screen has brought us both Bambi and Rambo. It makes our heroes and sometimes our presidents. It tells us what is in and what is out. It instructs our teenagers about sex, drugs, and rock n' roll. It teaches us how to dress, talk, and spit. It educates us about history:

- ☛ How Shakespeare really wrote Romeo and Juliet;
- ☛ Who really killed J.F.K.;
- ☛ How the Native American Indians really picked on the helpless cowboys;
- ☛ Who really invented the "smiley" face;
- ☛ How Jesus fooled everybody with the God disguise.

Hollywood is not only our cultural mentor, but our spiritual guide. Really.

Whatever you believe about the merits of Hollywood, there remains little dispute about the dominant role it plays in contemporary culture. The tragic element of this equation is the fact that non-Christians are not the only ones who turn to the gods of film for advice and consent. Christians appear just as eager as pagans to line-up for the Academy Awards. We, too, worship at Oscar's feet. We, too, are starstruck. We, too, dig the Hollywood presentation. We have embraced the attitude.

When pressed about the negative influence it has exercised on American manners, Hollywood collectively pleads innocence. "We don't shape culture," it maintains, "we only reflect and chronicle it."

Oh, yeah?

Then who popularized divorce, changing love from *agape* to *eros?* Who made sex a random act? Who made adultery a class act? Who made homosexuality a viable option? Who opened the closet? Who made Harry dirty? Who mainstreamed violence and carnage? Who fuels the movement to stomp out authority? Who made Madonna an idol? Who gives Barbara Streisand a political platform? Who authenticates New Age religious shenanigans? Who taught us to dance dirty? Who taught us not to give a damn? Who taught us to talk trash? Who taught us how to marry a millionaire? Who brought us Rosemary's Baby? Who cultivates nihilism? Who elevates con artists? Who encourages and legitimizes greed and avarice? Who debunked the notion that mankind can only find redemption in Jesus?

Hollywood, that's who.

No, thank you very much.

"Oh, lighten up, it's just entertainment," you are presently whispering under your breath. "You exaggerate the influence of Hollywood. They only reflect and chronicle culture. Stop making it sound evil. Prude."

Oh, yeah?

Remember that "Satan disguises himself as an angel of light" (2 Corinthians 11:14). The light is brightest in Hollywood. The Master Tempter plays with your mind. He deceives you by calling evil good and darkness light. He sneaks up on you. He subtracts biblical morals one at a time in hopes you won't notice. He infiltrates the best media of the day and deletes their innocence. He tells you everything is okay and then smacks you alongside the head when you aren't looking. He tries to extract God from the picture. He softens you up in subtle and insidious ways, and then closes in for the kill. That's entertainment!

The church has got to get out of Hollywood. What sense is there in staying? Get on I-10 East and head for the desert! Hollywood is naming and maiming us and our children. It may be part of the city of angels, but there ain't many heavenly angels left, and my guess is that those who remain feel like the ones who went to Sodom to rescue Lot (Genesis 19). Find a new address. Get a new attitude. Get out of town!

How about leaving H-O-L-L-Y-W-O-O-D for H-O-L-Y-W-O-O-D?

There is a lot more than an "L's" difference.

As obedient children, do not be conformed to the former lusts which were yours in your ignorance, but like the Holy One who called you, be holy yourselves also in all your behavior (1 Peter 1:14-15).

But you are a chosen race, a royal priesthood, a holy nation, a people for God's own possession, that you may proclaim the excellencies of Him who called you out of darkness into His marvelous light (1 Peter 2:9).

Live the rest of the time in the flesh no longer for the lusts of men, but for the will of God (1 Peter 4:2).

Do not be yoked together with unbelievers. For what do righteousness and wickedness have in common? Or what fellowship can light have with darkness? What is there between Christ and Belial? What does a believer have in common with an unbeliever? What agreement is there between the temple of God and idols? For we are the temple of the living God. As God has said, 'I will live with them and walk among them, and I will be their God, and they will be my people. Therefore come out from them and be separate, says the Lord. Touch no unclean thing, and I will receive you. I will be a Father to you, and you will be my sons and daughters, says the Lord Almighty' (2 Corinthians 6:14-18, NIV).

Cheat to Lose

Grandmothers represent the best of the species. They are wiser, kinder, and softer than regular humans. They hear more, see more, feel more, and believe more than folks with lesser years and fewer scars. Whereas common folks are burdened by gravity and defeat, grandmothers glide through life like a wind-powered hawk on a perfect spring afternoon. They are magically spared the constraints enforced on mere mortals.

Idiosyncrasies are easier to accept in grandmothers. If people of lesser stature acted like grandmothers, their behavior would be embarrassing. But weird is okay for grandmothers. They have earned the right to be a little odd. They play by a different set of rules.

My grandmother was no exception. Her cotton print dresses seldom fit correctly. Her glass jewelry was loud and funky, at times violating the senses and cursing contemporary fashion. She never carried a wallet. Instead she crammed currency and receipts in her bra. She laughed loudly and cried easily, both emotions prompting her to pull a wrinkled white hanky with red lace trim from the other side of her bra and gently dab the tears before they smeared the rouge strategically positioned high on her cheeks.

More concerned with function than style, she was seldom

seen at high profile social events—unless of course, one considers Saturday night bingo the stuff of society page puffery. She was politically incorrect before it was fashionable. Her language was salty and her similes came straight from the farm. Grandkids were silly as a goose, dull as a hoe, clever as a fox, straight as a board, stubborn as a mule, dirty as a pig, crazy as a peach orchard boar, finer than frog hair, and big as a barn. Grandma was a charter member of "Hee-Haw."

A simple woman, she lived one day at a time, finding beauty and meaning in the tasks at hand. Especially if the task had something to do with food. Granny loved food. She loved to grow it. Loved to prepare it. Loved to cook it. Loved to eat it. She was more concerned with weight for desirable women than desirable weight for women. Eating was her favorite indoor sport. She never fell prey to a gimmick diet. She never understood why someone might "want to lose thirty pounds in thirty days."

For thirty years Grandma cooked in a school cafeteria, baking bread, frying chicken, roasting beast, and disguising vegetables. It was there on a lean budget that she discovered the true secret to great recipes—bacon grease and brown sugar. With Granny's cooking no one worried about taking cholesterol supplements. Her meals stuck to your ribs . . . and your thighs and your tummy and your backside.

After retirement Grandma was seduced by a local cafe, and for another decade she spent five mornings a week crafting breakfast specials for a hungry crowd. They knew quality when they tasted it.

By the time I remember Grandma, she was retired again and spent most of her time at home—in the kitchen. We went to her house nearly every weekend to visit and eat. And play cards. Grandma's idea of a perfect day was to finish the dishes, snuggle into her big chair, and engage one of the grandkids in a friendly card game. She could play hour after hour and never tire. She knew dozens of different games. Her candy bowl was full of change in case there was interest in a little wagering.

It must have been the gene pool, because I loved to play cards with granny. By the time I was eight years old and had a thousand games under my belt, I had the intuitive feeling that Grandma conveniently changed the rules as we went along. Every time I would call her on it, I got the same response: "I'm just playing according to Hoyle."

I had no idea who or what Hoyle was, but she made it sound authoritative, and I humbly submitted to her questionable interpretation of the rules. Cooks are always the boss.

Years later I was buying a book at the variety store when I happened to stumble on a selection titled *Card Game Rules According to Hoyle*. I couldn't believe it! Hoyle was a guy. He wrote a book. Grandma was his disciple!

I bought it.

There were problems. Grandma's rules were often different than Mr. Hoyle's!

The next Saturday I hid the book in my shirt and went to Granny's house for lunch and cards. It was only the second hand of the afternoon when Granny pulled a fast one on me.

"Why did you do that, Granny?" I asked. "Last week you said it was just the opposite." "Ah, be quiet," she responded in typical fashion. "I'm just playing according to Hoyle."

The timing was perfect. I retrieved the manual from my shirt, opened to page 37 and began to quote the rules. Granny's false teeth bounced off the table. "Where did you get that?"she demanded to know.

"The jig is up, Granny. You're busted," I smiled.

From that day on we played according to Hoyle. And I regularly got trounced. It seems that Granny cheated at cards for those many years so I could win more than I lost! She gambled and lost so I could have some coins to jingle in my pocket. The day we started playing fairly was the day she began beating me to a pulp, though still with her big smile in tact.

Granny cheated to make sure her special little grandson won more than he lost. She wanted him confident and secure through controlled successes so he would be ready to meet the cruel realities of a cold world as a man. She played cards with bacon grease and brown sugar. She played life so others could win.

Early on Grandma taught me that I don't want what I deserve. I don't want justice or fairness. I want grace. I want someone else to shuffle the cards so I get all the aces. It doesn't have to make sense, I just want to win.

Perhaps our experiences with granny-type folks help us to appreciate what God has done for us in the atoning sacrifice of Jesus. With salvation we get what we don't deserve. God trounced Satan on our behalf. Jesus cheated Satan out of our souls. We deserve to die for our sins, but instead "God sent his only Son into the world, that whoever believes in him should not die, but have eternal life" (John 3:16).

But God demonstrates His own love toward us, in that while we were yet sinners, Christ died for us (Romans 5:8).

But God, being rich in mercy, because of His great love with which He loved us, even when we were dead in our transgressions, made us alive together with Christ (by grace you have been saved) (Ephesians 2:4,5).

Perhaps Psalm 103 says it best:

The Lord is compassionate and gracious,
Slow to anger and abounding in lovingkindness.
He will not always strive with us;
Nor will He keep His anger forever.
He has not dealt with us according to our sins,
Nor rewarded us according to our iniquities.
For as high as the heavens are above the earth,
So great is His lovingkindness toward those who fear Him.
As far as the east is from the west,
So far has He removed our transgressions from us.
Just as a father has compassion on his children,
So the Lord has compassion on those who fear Him.
For He himself knows our frame;
He is mindful that we are but dust.

Chalk Up
Another One

Running from his past was nothing new for Wayne Parker. He had been doing it all his life. But this time, things would be different—he hoped.

Wayne rolled into Dallas a few years ago, a wake of destruction trailing close behind. Frustrated by his troubles and inability to do the right thing, he decided to change . . . his name. Wayne consistently messed up everything he touched, so Wayne ditched Wayne and became Lloyd. Perhaps Lloyd could stay out of trouble.

No such luck. Lloyd was not any better than Wayne. New name, same old problems. "It was frustrating," Lloyd confessed, "I quickly discovered that Lloyd had brought Wayne with him. He and me had the same problems."

Lloyd now readily admits that his past was not the only thing from which he was running: "I was running from God. Years ago I had 'tuned in and dropped out,' but I dropped out so far that I was in another universe." For decades Lloyd (really Wayne) had done his own thing, thinking he could somehow operate independently of God and mainline civility. He failed on every front, and something inside of him began to scream: "There has to be more to life than what I have experienced!"

It was a strange set of events that brought Wayne (really

Lloyd) to the Central Dallas Ministries' building in East Dallas. "Basically I was in between crimes and bored," he testified before a spellbound breakfast crowd recently. "I was looking for an easy place to rip off and I went to scope the joint!"

Fellow volunteers put him to work stacking vegetable cans in the food pantry. He worked all morning and then a unique thing happened. They asked him to come back. "I had never been asked back before," he laughed. "I didn't know how to respond."

He came back the next day. And the next. And the next. He showed up faithfully all week, and then the preacher from the Central Dallas Church of Christ invited him to come to church on Sunday. Their kindness made no earthly sense.

Stunned by the attention, he agreed. "Lost my senses," he quipped. There he met Jesus and found what he had been searching for all his life. "It was love, man, unconditional love. All my life I had been looking for love, and I found it at Central."

In his confession and testimony before the church, Lloyd bared his soul. "I came here to rob you blind, and Jesus stole my heart."

Today Lloyd has a real job and real hope. He finally buried Wayne—once and for all. Chalk up another one for the love of God: the irresistible, unconditional, life-changing love of God.

The Bible comes to life when folks like Lloyd come to Jesus. The born again experience shifts from spiritual theory to material reality. "Therefore if any man is in Christ, he is a new creature; the old things passed away; behold, new things have come" (2 Corinthians 5:17). Encountering real live, flesh and blood, born-again converts reminds us that God has the power and the desire to make all things new! Welcome, Lloyd, to the grace club!

God is in the redeeming business. He delights in transforming darkness into light. Even when all the king's horses and all the king's men can't put Humpty together again, God can reassemble the pieces and restore what is broken. In a world of broken dreams, broken hearts, broken backs, and broken lives, the tender and compassionate hands of God move to heal the broken spirit. "Blessed are those who are poor in Spirit" (Matthew 5:3).

Churches must constantly keep in mind (and heart) the true nature of their constituency. Church ain't a place for perfect people. Church is the place where imperfect people grow in their pursuit of God's righteousness. Church is a journey. And we are all travelers along the highway called life. You, I, and Lloyd are fellow pilgrims, united in spirit and Spirit, trekking toward heaven together. **Church is the great expedition.**

We dare not leave the likes of Lloyd behind.

Church must be a safe place for folks like Wayne/Lloyd. We are not a private country club trying to keep out the riff-raff. Instead, we are out gathering lost souls (like Jesus: see Matthew 8 & 9). Church isn't impressed by worldly success or cultural alignment. You don't have to have it all together to come to church.

Establishments with a history of suspect patronage often display a warning label over the bar that states, "We reserve the right to refuse service to anyone."

In direct contrast, church sense dictates that we ought to hang a big sign above our front door declaring, "We reserve the right to accept everyone!"

The church is in the redeeming business (it is in the spiritual gene pool; we inherit it from God). Sinners don't have to pre-qualify to get a reserved seat. It has nothing to do with luck. All are welcome. While the world culls its patrons and divides folks into acceptable and unacceptable camps, the church trails behind gathering up the misfits and rejects.

The church is "loser-friendly." After all, we serve a "loser-friendly" Savior. We receive losers because we are fellow losers, and we are all accepted by God. None of us—thank God—get what we deserve (please reread Psalm 103)! Does this "loser-friendly" stuff mean we endorse sin? Nope. It simply means we love the sinner because the "love of Christ controls us" (2 Corinthians 5:14, NASB). Remember, this is Christ's church. And we are his "ministers of reconciliation" (2 Corinthians 5:18-21).

It's great to be part of a church that majors in acceptance, hope, and renewal. Maybe Lloyd will show up for a visit.

Bert the Bus
Is a Lot Like Us

I adopted Bert in the early spring of 1982. His former owner had abandoned him on an old logging road a few miles above Newman Lake, Washington. I found him laying on his side in a snow bank, unconscious and suffering from hypothermia, but with a pulse.

Bert was a 1961 GMC school bus, one of the world's premier examples of mechanical wizardry. He was created back in the days when they really knew how to make them. No plastic. No aluminum. No space age compounds concerned with strength-to-weight ratios. Bert the bus featured steel. And steel dies hard.

Weighing more than a ship full of Japanese imports, Bert was tired but not worn out. He still had some miles left in him.

I sent a truck ambulance to the mountain and they towed the carcass to town. I put him in the shop, and as his parts began to thaw, color returned to his fenders. Within a week he was off life support and breathing on his own. I told my wife that he had followed me home for dinner.

My goal in this whole rehabilitation process was to get Bert healthy enough to move us to Dallas. Not all of us were convinced that Bert was up to the task. Sandra suggested that we might instead consider employing the services of a moving company. I rejected the idea—too orthodox, too reasonable, too expensive, too female.

"Look at Bert," I told her. "He can do it!"

"Why don't you look at Bert?" she responded. "He isn't much to look at." Then she gave me "that" look.

She had a point.

He looked a little haggard. He was the bus of many colors: yellow, white, red, and rust. Previous owners had painted Bert to their liking, and now the extremes of weather and neglect had blended the brush jobs into a tapestry of colors. Only the factory yellow was consistent. His appearance was complicated by a lack of medical attention. Many of his cuts and scrapes had never been stitched. A few open wounds oozed pus that detracted from his overall presentation. Graffiti also suggested that not all of the children who had ridden in Bert were from good homes. A few years prior, a fancy little foreign beast had tried to get cute with Bert and some of the remains protruded from his grill. A visit to the coast on another occasion had left a serious scar on the upper left side of the cabin. Rumor was that a Douglas Fir had mugged the bus and stolen the mirror, clearance lights, and decorative trim. It had been awhile since he had seen a professional groomer.

In contrast to the colorful adjectives employed by Sandra, I chose to think of Bert as "experienced." His speedometer had retired and started drawing social security at a half-million hard miles. The muffler no longer muffled. The tires all held air; it wasn't important that all six had different tread designs (what do you expect from recaps?). A homeless swallow had built a nest in the fresh air vent and several windows were creatively tinted.

Bert had no air conditioning, compact disc player, onboard computer analysis, six-way adjustable driver's seat, electric locks, or child restraining seats. The windshield wiper was wiped out, the right blinker was on the blink, the horn was philosophically opposed to honking, the gauges refused to leave home base, and the safety sticker had been purchased on the black market. But he had a great personality.

Bert got six miles per gallon—city or country, uphill or down, leaded or unleaded. The oil consumption was marginally less, and yes, you could see the exhaust. But he started every time without fail, and once you got him moving, he was hard to stop (did I mention the brakes were broken?).

I cut a deal with Sandra. I drove the bus to Dallas. She and the children followed at a safe distance. We had periodic contact. I parked the bus across the street from the motel. When I was detained by local authorities, they waved and waited down the road.

But we made it! Two years later we turned around and did it again. This time the boys rode with me. They thought Bert was cool. Plus I had the cooler.

I learned a lot from Bert the Bus. For you see, "Bert the Bus is a lot like us."

All he really needed was a little TLC, someone to love his old bones and groom his chassis. Buses differ little from people; they both need attention, affirmation, care, and a chance to prove themselves. Love covers a multitude of miles.

In many ways Bert reminds me of the church as described in Romans 12 and 1 Corinthians 12. Paul uses the human body to draw an analogy to the function of the church body, graphically illustrating how each part of the body is important to its overall function. The body needs all its parts to run like God created it.

Bert the Bus serves as a similar illustration. Bert weighed eight tons, but if you removed a two-ounce coil wire he was paralyzed. Every component in Bert's inventory was important. Some parts looked and acted more important, but they were all interdependent on one another. Spark plugs and wheels each had a role. Bert made good church sense.

During the month that I doctored Bert, I grew in appreciation for the function of each part. Everything had a place.

For just as we have many members in one body and all the members do not have the same function, so we, who are many, are one body in Christ, and individually members one of another (Romans 12:4,5).

Just because you are not a transmission or a steering wheel, don't think that you are not an important part of the body. And if you are the big-shot onboard computer, then "do not think more highly of yourself than you ought" (Romans 12:3, NIV).

Discover your function (gift, talent, interest) and become the best part you can be! The church can't run without you.

Subluxated, Marinated, and Violated

I know something about physical pain.

I've had seven hip surgeries, two knee surgeries, fourteen sets of stitches, one kidney stone (too many), one tonsillectomy, eleven jammed fingers (make that ten), one dislocated shoulder (found weeks later vacationing in Santa Fe), seven smashed fingernails, a deep thigh bruise, two sprained ankles that made me cry, a half-dozen black eyes (broadcasting when I should have been tuning in), numerous split lips and personalities, and indigestion from too many late night burritos. I've had adolescent growing pains, seasonal migrating headaches, frequent mental pause, an annoying case of male pattern baldness, obvious half-heimers, and a tidy little frontal lobotomy to keep life in perspective.

Malady is my middle name.

I have been used, abused, and confused; spindled, torn, and crumpled; tattooed, glued, and screwed; dipped, ripped, and zipped; subluxated, marinated, and violated; decootered, retutored, and roto-rootered; smeared, tiered, and jeered. I've had tennis elbow, pain transfer, and key lime disease. I've had hangnails, hangerons, and killer hangovers. I've had cysts removed and used parts installed. I've had numerous prostheses, contheses, and late night, desperate talks with Jesus. I have some parts that don't wake up some mornings.

I've abused Demerol, Naprosin, codeine, adrenaline and Jack Daniels®. I've battled melancholy funny bones, foolish wisdom teeth, and a deviated septum now gone straight. I've experienced motion sickness as well as Still's Disease. I've been up all night with earaches, headaches, toothaches, and heartaches. I've been bitten by dogs, cats, bees, fire ants, women, and small children.

Hurt here. Hurt there. Hurt everywhere. I've earned my handicap sticker.

I know something about hospitals, too. And doctors' offices. Read every issue of "Field and Spleen." Clinics. Ambulances. Psych wards. I've had my head examined, my feet massaged, my ears lowered, my privates made public, and my prostate checked—but only once! I've shared hospital rooms with winos, whiners, wimps, pimps, punks, psychopaths, pickers, grinners, and hypochondriacs. I've befriended folks who suffered from yellow jaundice, gangrene, black plague, pink eye, red spots, and scarlet letters. I blacked-out once in recovery. Saw Elvis. Hustled back. I kindly beat up the pervert who invented the hospital gown, the worthless pond scum who stole my last ounce of dignity. I've been sterilized, cauterized, catheterized, anesthetized, injected, rejected, projected, bedpanned, CAT-scanned, dog-tired, haywired, X-rayed, examined, examinated, pollinated, and manipulated.

I've had paralysis by analysis. I've been malpracticed, practiced on, and practically destroyed. I've had more bad diagnoses than Carter has liver pills. Been to Parkland Hospital. Barely survived it. I've fought with belligerent insurance companies—the gypsies, tramps, and thieves. I've eaten the cafeteria's worst grease bombs—with friends like this, who needs enemas? I've given birth to twins (not really, just trying to empathize with female readers). I send monthly payments to four different hospitals, six different doctors, five sundry specialists, plus some clinic in New Jersey that drew my name at random. I've played with fire, sharp instruments, and teenage sons. Got hurt each time.

But I'm not complaining.

Pain is my friend. I've learned and grown through the pain. Pain has been very, very good to me.

It is easy to underestimate the value of pain. Pity the person who lives pain-free. They know little of the beauty and power of compassion.

The best thing about pain is that it can be shared. Like a rich chocolate malt for two or a seat on the ferris wheel, pain is better when shared among friends. Life was not designed to hurt alone. We are manufactured by God to bear one another's burdens and relieve one another's pain. Pain is not senseless.

Life has a cyclic flavor. At times we are strong and pain-free and God uses us to minister to others. At other times we are broken and hurt and need the charitable kindness of a brother or sister. In both scenarios we grow closer to one another. Sympathy covers a multitude of pains.

Hospitals are great places, hotbeds for mercy and goodness. Healing given; healing received. No pharmaceutical wonder drug has the power of human care and prayer.

Churches are hospitals of a sort, only better. Church is the place where broken hearts, broken lives, and broken dreams are mended. Church is the place where charity and compassion know no limits.

Church is a hospital for pain-riddled sinners—like you and me.

It Ain't
Rocket Science

After nearly forty years of serious rocket science, many of them spent on the deserted white sands of New Mexico, Harvey Widner retired.

"It was a no-brainer decision," he told me. "It didn't take a rocket scientist to figure out it was time to go."

"Were you always a rocket scientist?" I asked.

"Basically," he responded, "but I had some odd jobs before I finished college."

"What was your very first job?"

"I remember it well. I grew up in farming country outside a little New Mexican town. I was twelve years old when I took a weekend job grubbing Johnson grass."

"How long did you work?"

"An hour and a half!"

"An hour and a half?"

"Yes, and it was an hour too long."

"I assume you didn't think much of your first job," I jabbed him.

"I hated it," he laughed.

"Why was it so bad?"

"The farmer took my cousin and me out into the middle of a

forty-acre field, handed us a grubbing hoe, and drove off. We worked for an hour and hadn't moved three feet. We figured it would take us the rest of our lives to finish the field."

"And you weren't interested?" I asked.

"We weren't interested!"

"So what did you do?"

"We quit. We walked back to the house and collected our seventy-five cents."

The nostalgic moment got Harvey giggling at his childhood exploits.

"I remember being absolutely overwhelmed. My hoe was so small and the field so big; my cousin and I decided we had no chance."

"Let me get this right," I interrupted. "Grubbing Johnson grass was too complicated so you became a rocket scientist instead?"

"That's right," he affirmed with a nod of his head. "I got into something I could handle."

Although I never grubbed grass, I know how Harvey felt. My first job was roguing peas. It is a similar vocation to grubbing. Both are grunt work best suited for teenagers with undeveloped brains. Adult type people don't rogue peas. They get someone else—like unsuspecting teens—to do their dirty work.

It works like this. Farmer Brown gives you a water jug, two sandwiches, the promise of a five o'clock pickup, and then dumps you off in the middle of a four thousand acre field and says, "Rogue, boy, rogue," as he smiles and drives off to the comfort of the farmhouse.

Plucking evil tares from the righteous plants is fun—for the first ten minutes. Then it is sheer hell under the blistering noonday sun. Minutes seem like hours. Hours seem like days. I rogued peas for two months the first two hours. Before lunch my stone cold heart was filled with hatred. Satan abused me. I cursed the curse, the rotten day Adam and Eve conscripted me into hard labor. Rogue weeds became killer weeds. It was me against them and the whole dark world. I cursed the farmer. His lovely wife. His fat dogs. His ugly tractor. His stupid, stinking, worthless herbicides. And my own stupidity.

I honed my cursing skills that day.

I wore out early. But I lasted longer than Harvey. Four hours longer. I stumbled back to the farmhouse at 2:00 and called Mom, pleading with her to come rescue her only son. I overwhelmed her with tears.

I whimpered all the way home. My hands hurt. My feet hurt. My back really hurt. My gall bladder hurt. My pride hurt.

It was not funny at the time. The worst day of my life and all I had to show for it was an ugly blister on my big toe and a dollar and sixty-five cents!

Reflecting on my rendition of the world's worst job, I remember that the physical pain and personal insult were not its worst features. Neither was the abject boredom or the sales calls from hell. The subhuman sandwich meat was terrible, as was the peanut bitter cookie, but they didn't drive me to quit.

The worst aspect of roguing peas, and grubbing Johnson grass for that matter, is the overwhelming sense of frustration with the size of the job at hand. If a zillion-acre field has a million zillion weeds, what good is it to pull a half dozen? Or a dozen? Or a good portion of a zillion? It's hard to start when you know you can't finish.

If farmers were smart (like preachers and rocket scientists), they would do things differently if they wanted their grunt work done by unsuspecting teens. If farmers asked my opinion, here is what I would tell them (there are a lot of *ifs* to this equation):

☛ Break your giant fields into little plots. Take a cue from Chinese sharecroppers. Put your valued employees (a new way of thinking about unsuspecting teens) into a situation they can master. Give them a hundred square feet at a time. Feed them (real people food), pat them on the back, and give them another plot. Watch them work! Listen to them whistle while they work! See them gad about as they whistle while they work!

☛ Provide them companionship while they work. Let them pass the time in the fellowship of other valued employees. Create performance teams with incentives and Christmas bonuses. Keep them busy so they don't notice the magnitude of the task. Help them understand they are having fun.

☛ Encourage them. Work with them. Freak them out by getting down on your knees and roguing a few peas. Eat lunch with them. Be a regular guy. Get a blister.

☛ Don't let them quit. Keep emphasizing the rewards. Tell them what they can do with their earnings. Nip cursing in the bud (I love agricultural metaphors). Tell their mothers not to come get them, even if they are crying, even if they are girls, even if they are tired, even if they quit. Make them hang in there. Endurance is the operative virtue.

I admit that these suggestions aren't rocket science, but I guarantee you they will work—in more fields than wheat or peas.

Consider the plight of the new Christian. In many ways they resemble an unsuspecting teen dropped in the middle of the King Ranch and told to start grubbing.

They are immediately overwhelmed. Everywhere they look there is more Johnson grass with no end in sight. They are given a little rusty hoe and admonished to make dust. No other worker is within shouting distance. Their lunchbox is in the back of the pickup truck that just disappeared over yonder horizon. They don't know where to start, much less where they are going. All they know is they had better look busy.

No wonder so many quit.

Maturing new Christians ain't rocket science. Instead it is biblical science—and art. It is just good church sense. It is encouragement, fellowship, instruction, praise, positive models, goals, promises, patience, empathy, perseverance, love, and the power of the Holy Spirit.

What kind of a farmer are you?

Extra Parts

There's no way I'm going to pay another $25 to buy one already assembled!"

"Please," Sandra pleaded, "it will be the cheapest $25 you'll ever spend."

"It's a waste of money," I objected. "Why should I pay someone else to do what I can handle myself?"

"I don't know how to tell you this," my wife of twenty-five years and twenty-five thousand strange experiences said, "but I'm not convinced you can handle it."

"Now why would you say something like that? I grew up on a stump ranch with a Crescent wrench for a pacifier. Remember, I was in the machinery business. I am blessed by God with mechanical sensibilities. I can put together this simple little Bar-B-Q. How hard can it be?"

She walked off shaking her head in disgust while I loaded the unassembled model onto the cart. "Don't worry, honey," I shouted up the aisle. "It will be a piece of cake! We'll be grilling steaks by dinner time!"

Anxious to prove my skeptic wife wrong, I brought the big, bad barbecue box into the kitchen, opened it, and dumped all the parts on the floor. I showed Sandra the cover of the instruction manual: "Assemble yourself with pliers and a screwdriver." I felt invigorated.

As soon as I located the section of the manual written in English, I began the assembly process. Piece of cake. The foot bone connected to the ankle bone. The ankle bone connected to the shin bone. The shin bone connected to the knee bone. . . . but then the thigh bone came up missing. I looked again through the pile of parts. Nothing.

Irritated, but still calm, I expressed a portion of my thoughts out loud. "How do they expect you to put this thing together when they forget to include all the parts?"

Irritated, but still calm, Sandra suggested I reinspect the manual for clarification. "Honey," I patiently explained to her, "you have to understand that this manual was written by an abused daughter of a communist general in a third-world country." The instructions lacked precision. Extra and unnecessary arrows had been added to confuse the end consumer. Parts in the book did not always resemble parts on the floor. I smiled. "Don't worry sweetheart, I'll figure it out without the manual."

She feigned a smile and went shopping. Left me home with the mess. It only added to my determination. I decided to *make* the parts fit. My boyhood training on the farm had taught me that the solution to most assembly problems was a bigger hammer and a hotter welder.

I worked on the grill all afternoon. Dinnertime came and went. The sun went down. My blood pressure went up. I created a thigh bone from my boneyard in the garage. A little black touch-up paint and no one would know the difference. The whole time I concentrated on the money I saved by doing it myself. A couple more cost-saving projects like this and I would be bankrupt or institutionalized.

About bedtime I snapped. I took the manual and ripped it into shreds. I stomped on the shreds. I gathered the shreds, took them outside, poured lighter fluid on them, and torched them. I felt better.

Then I went and found Sandra. I showed her the completed project and begged for affirmation. "I told you I could do it. Isn't it beautiful? And look, only forty-four parts left over!"

I know it is exactly forty-four parts because I just recounted them a few minutes ago. They are in a sandwich bag on my desk.

I'm considering sending them back to the manufacturer for a refund. But I can't find an address. And the instruction manual is missing.

I am still angry. Why can't we get a president and a congress that will draft trade laws that would stop foreign conspirators from importing products with perverted instruction manuals? For instance, they should draft a law that requires all manuals to make sense. Now there is an idea! We could follow up with a law that fines shady importers $1,000 for each extra part. Why would you send a backyard grill across seven oceans with forty-four extra parts? Somebody ought to pay! Perhaps the most effective legislation would hold the author of the instruction manual personally accountable. If the manual cannot be interpreted by an American male of average intelligence and spunk, then the writer ought to be bound in a public stockade and pelted with extra parts, with the offended casting the first wing nut.

Take my wife's advice. Pay the $25! It is the sensible thing to do.

I hate to admit it, but I suppose there are people out there who can actually decipher the secret codes of a technical product manual. Unlike the rest of us, they are not intimidated by the complexities of a simple process. With years of experience, they have familiarized themselves with the unique language and customs of the big, bad instruction manual. I'm impressed, but I hope I never have to read enough of them to join the club.

It has occurred to me that many of our neighbors feel the same way about the Bible—the great instruction manual for life. We forget that most Kingdomites cut our teeth on Bible stories and have spent our lives interpreting the manual. We've cultivated our church sense. For committed Bible students it is easy to forget that not everyone is as familiar with Scripture as we are.

Reality testifies that many folks consider the Bible to be a complicated manual authored by a foreign source unfamiliar with contemporary practices, culture, or language. It doesn't make sense. To them it is a collection of secret codes and formulas that cannot be deciphered by the average person. They are intimidated by it. So most ignore it.

Perhaps the biggest favor we can do for our neighbors is to

help them read and understand the Bible. It doesn't come pre-assembled. They will have to put it together by themselves, and they will need some help. Why not grab a pair of pliers, a screwdriver, and a concordance and walk across the street to give your neighbors a hand in constructing their lives? It will go a lot better if they can read the manual.

Remember the Alamo

hat were you thinking?" Sandra asked me when I told her about our 6 a.m. round-about flight to Los Angeles.

"I was thinking we saved fifty bucks," I responded, now suddenly on the defense and backpedaling.

"Do you know what time we will have to get up to be at the airport on time?" There was an edge to her tone.

"Early?"

"About 4 a.m. early," she lectured me. "About two hours earlier than any human being should have to face the day."

"But we saved fifty bucks," I reminded her, hoping that her frugal leanings would prevail.

"Spend it on coffee," she said. "We'll need it."

Airline flights that depart before sunrise often spell trouble. It is an unnatural thing to do. Airplanes are sleepy. Pilots are disoriented. Attendants are grouchy. Baggage handlers will bite your head off if you look at them wrong. Fellow passengers are edgy; couples traveling together argue over who was the idiot who made these ridiculous reservations.

Our day came. We got up, got dressed, got going, and got to DFW at 5:30. I dropped Sandra off with the bags at the TWA gate and circled around to find a parking spot (I figured at this time of morning she was a match for the baggage handler.).

When I walked out of the garage toward the gate, I saw my lovely wife on the curb with the bags.

"What's up, honey?" I inquired.

"There is no 6 a.m. flight," she smiled. "It was canceled two months ago."

I looked at the fellow with the big hat and the big frown and asked if it was true.

"There has been no flight to St. Louis (another reason I saved fifty bucks) this time of morning since before Christmas."

"But I've got the tickets right here," I protested, "they say 6 a.m."

"They may say 6 a.m., and it may be 6 a.m., and you may have saved fifty bucks, but there ain't no 6 a.m. flight."

He was very persuasive.

"Well," I said, "what do you think we ought to do?"

"If I were you, I'd go upstairs and talk to a TWA agent." As we turned to follow his instructions, he spoke again, "but I wouldn't expect much help, especially this early in the morning."

We waited at the counter until the arrival of an agent a few minutes after six. She snapped the tickets from my hand and shook her head. "You have a problem," she lamented.

I was hoping she would say, "*We* have a problem." This was not a problem of which I was seeking ownership.

"Tell you what I can do," she said. "How about a 9:35 a.m. flight on American?"

I nodded in approval. Sandra nodded louder.

We marched our bags out of the terminal and after a brief search and rescue mission found my truck. We drove to the American terminal and I dropped Sandra and the bags off while I found a place to park. I took note of the location.

Different guy, same song, second verse. We took our bags and our pain and went to the American Airlines counter. There we stood in line for a long time. When our turn finally came, I handed the growing collection of ticket stuff to the agent, and she performed the patented negative head shake, a trait employed by various folks working behind counters dealing with stupid customers before sunrise.

"What a mess," she commented. "Do you often fly this early?"

"Never again," Sandra responded.

"Just trying to save a few a bucks," I added.

Both women shook their heads in disgust.

"Now take your heavy bags down there about a half-mile or so and get them x-rayed," she instructed us. "And if they pass inspection, we might let you on the plane!"

"Well, whoopee," I whispered under my breath, afraid to cross her.

The plane left on time and we were on it.

We touched down in Ontario, California, and when I looked out the window, the terminal was abandoned. A few minutes later we discovered they had built a whole new airport since our last visit to Los Angeles. "Whoopee," I whispered under my breath.

I eventually located and secured a spot on the shuttle to the Rent-a-Car satellite location. I left Sandra with the bags and promised a quick return. "What else could go wrong?" I encouraged her, "We're home free."

After a thirty-minute wait in the Alamo line, I found out what else could go wrong. They had no record of a Carlson reservation. The place was packed and cars were gone. The Alamo agent lamented my incompetence. But for $89 a day and a second-round draft choice, he could put me in a sleek used compact, like a Geo® or a Corvair®.

It was before noon, left coast time, but I was exhausted. It had already been a full day and my hassle quotient had been reached.

Then suddenly my life changed. Out of the back room stepped Dale Carnegie's lost nephew.

"What seems to be the problem here?" he asked Mister Behind-the-Counter.

"Mr. Carlson claims he has a reservation, but Mr. Carlson is mistaken."

Mr. Carlson's temperature elevated several more degrees.

"I doubt that," Mr. Friendly said. "Mr. Carlson doesn't look like the kind of man to be mistaken."

I liked this guy.

"Let me handle this one," he said as he brushed Mr. Matter-of-Fact out of the way.

"How would you like to save fifty bucks, Mr. Carlson?" he asked me.

"I'd like that very much," I smiled.

"How would you like to have a big luxury car for the weekend for say, oh, $25.99 a day?"

"Mrs. Carlson would be very pleased, too," I told him. He sensed I needed the points.

"To do this," he said, "we have to have a reservation. But that's no problem. Do you know a travel agent anywhere that you can call who will make you a reservation over the Internet? Here, use our phone. Dial "9" to get an outside line. Can I get you a cup of coffee while you are dialing?"

I had no sooner hung up when he handed back my credit card.

"Look's like we'll have to put you in a brand new car. Is that satisfactory, Mr. Carlson?"

"Yeah," I stammered, "that will work."

"You don't mind if I throw in a full tank of gas and a map, do you?"

Stunned, but still coherent, I nodded affirmingly. He mirrored the action. First person I had seen behind a counter whose head moved up and down.

"I'll have a fellow bring it up front in just a moment," he said as he handed me the keys. "Have a nice day, Mr. Carlson, and I hope the Mrs. likes the car."

"Oh, she will," I responded with a complimentary smile, "and wait 'til she hears I saved fifty bucks!"

I can't express how delighted I was to encounter Mr. PMA. He was an absolute breath of fresh air. He wanted to help. He wanted my business. He wanted my wife to like me. He wanted to make a difference.

Because of the positive efforts of one man, I will always "remember the Alamo." From now on, I'm renting from Alamo, even if I don't save fifty bucks. I want to go where the customer is always right.

One positive person can make a huge difference.

Is that one person you?

Sadly, many of us have a "behind-the-counter" mentality. We're just not very friendly. Our presentation often has a negative edge. It's bad for business, but more importantly, it's bad for Christianity. To top it off, it is plain bad church sense.

How is your Christian presentation? Do you want to impress someone with your faith? Then put a smile on your face and act like you're saved! Be kind. Be helpful. Be friendly. Be encouraging. Be nice. Move your head up and down. Save somebody fifty bucks. Save somebody from a bad day. Save somebody from hell. Prove you have a good church sense.

The church needs to drive the world crazy with its friendliness: friendliness to those who don't want it, don't expect it, don't deserve it. Love them anyway. Serve them anyway. Save them anyway.

Numbskulls
on the Loose

M y friend grew up in a church where he heard the same message every Sunday morning: *"God loves you, and you are going to hell."* He quit going when he grew up.

A fine lady came back to church recently after a thirty-five year absence. She and her husband had been disfellowshipped in 1965 for irregular attendance. She decided it was safer not to go at all.

I visited with a fellow recently who is looking for a new church home because the preacher at his ex-congregation said he would rather have his children watch a XXX pornographic video than the television show: *Touched by an Angel.* He thinks the preacher is touched in the head. Another not-so-popular area preacher publicly declared that he would "Rather be exposed to HIV than the NIV!" I hope he is not contagious.

"God's grace sent Jesus from heaven to the cross, but you have to get yourself from the cross to heaven," was the signature sermon of the preacher where another of my confused friends used to attend church. He has not done real well getting himself to heaven. He thinks it makes more sense to try to link up with the grace that brought Jesus here in the first place.

I ran into an ex-preacher at a Chinese restaurant last week.

He is still stinging from a church bite nearly a decade ago. His wife ran off with another man and they fired *him* because he made them look bad. He got a double divorce for the price of one. And he didn't want either. He is in no mood for reconciliation.

A preacher friend of mine has got a mess on his hands. A small but obnoxious group of legalists in his congregation has decided that a person's conversion is not authentic if he/she does not prove his/her genuineness of repentance by restoring all the wrongs of his/her pagan journey. It seems they are not so much concerned with returning a stolen watch to Dillard's or paying an old veterinarian bill as they are dumping a current spouse if you have been married once before. You heard it right. They are saying that God can forgive any sin but divorce and remarriage. They advocate the only way you can descend the baptismal steps is to put away your current mate and return to the bliss of your first marriage (because your ex-spouse will obviously dump his/her current mate to take you back to satisfy the church's demand). Holy headache, Batman!

A big theological debate is scheduled for the near future where two learned men will wrangle over the correctness of eating a meal in a church building that has been paid for (the meal, not the building) by money extracted from the general church fund. Thank God one man is denying the proposition! Parking is not limited. Tickets are available. Good seats remain. The future of Christianity hangs in the balance.

Thirty-seven million unborn babies slaughtered in America in the last thirty-seven years and we debate how to pay for lunch? Millions of people dying every year without knowing Jesus, and we have the gall to worry about the theology of contraband Spam® in the foyer? Racism and hedonism and shedonism are ripping our culture apart, and we focus on the scriptural authority for appliances? Would it not be better to focus on stuff for which God gives a flip—like souls?

A small church (not only in numbers, but in mercy, ministry, and common church sense) in rural Texas recently took dramatic steps to keep the church body pure from liberal thinking. They fired the preacher. At a Wednesday night men's business meeting, he requested a new overhead projector. It was denied and justified by a brother who declared, "The Bible says to do things in ancient ways and there is no such thing as an overhead projector mentioned anywhere." Now *there* is a saint who knows the Book. The preacher got out of town before they tarred and feathered him.

I was once caught up into the third heaven and saw a vision of a missionary who had his support cut off for distributing the New International Version of the Bible. "It's heretical," they told him, "published by denominationalists who believe in the Holy Spirit." He tried to reason with them, but to no avail. "You sound like one of those Holy Spirit nuts, too," they told him. And they took his travel funds, too. That will teach him, too.

A family left a church last year because they believed that the evanglist believed that folks who believed in Jesus but did not believe exactly like *they* believed still had a chance to be believers in God's sight. It freaked them out. They returned to the safety of their old church where folks believe like they are supposed to believe. And like nobody else believes.

A number of years ago I attended a modern day Pharisaical convention. It was awesome. I came away with a perfect example of how not to think, act, or be. I was taught all kinds of valuable skills: like how to be small, petty, backward, dishonest, irregular, and numbskullish. I rejoice that the council continues to shrink, not surprising since they themselves draw the circle smaller and the noose tighter.

I thank God that I belong to a church where, *"God loves me, and I am going to heaven!"* I am glad that we have created a church environment where people want to meet regularly. Isn't it great not to be afraid to be "touched by an angel?" Blessed Assurance! God sent Jesus and God called me! Grace has brought me safe thus far, and grace will lead me home. Because God loves us, he hates our destructive behavior, including divorce. But we serve a God who forgives our sins in Jesus' name and "as far as the east is from the west, so far has He removed our transgressions from us" (Psalm 103:12). God forgives and forgets. So can we! Church is a hotbed of forgiveness.

Every good and perfect gift is from God—given for us to enjoy. God feeds His people and tells us to enjoy his generous provision. It is a joyous event to break bread with brethren every-where—in homes, restaurants, and fellowship halls. Pass the butter, brother!

I love Bible study. I love noble brethren who study the Bible to learn God's will, not reinforce traditions or human creeds. And I love the freedom to study it for myself without councils or Grand Mucketymucks interpreting their brand of truth. Thanks for letting me study and learn firsthand. A church that studies honestly together stays together.

Fellowship in the Spirit paces the Christian walk. We want to be Spirit led. Who in their right mind would want to be human led? Life in the Spirit is love and peace and gentleness and joy and hope. May we unite and lose our identity in the Spirit of God.

Thank you, God, for delivering us from the frailties of our human condition and equipping us with power from on high. We praise your name and we exalt your church!

Well, I'll Be Go to Hell

His daddy, crippled from the Korean War, could not work. His mama never saw forty. They were burned to death in a trailer house fire. Bob somehow escaped the inferno, but he was on his own at sixteen, a tragedy waiting to happen. He is nearly fifty now—his mama would be proud.

He has been an alcoholic, drug addict, vagabond, and purveyor of trouble. The Railroad canned him a decade ago because he was trouble . . born on the wrong side of the tracks. He spent the '80s in Las Vegas working the strip and following the pattern of the dark side. The '90s were worse. He peddled cocaine for fun and profit, lived on the ragged edge, often dangling precariously from a broken branch above the fiery pit. He never married. One of the few things he did right. No reason to ruin two lives. A streetwise and blindly loyal Irish Setter was his only steady companion. Bad dog.

I left his seamy world in the late '70s and by the grace of God tried to straighten up my own act. I never saw him again—until recently. He called out of the blue one night to say he was straight, off the cocaine and the lam. He told me he loved me, missed his old buddy. I knew he meant it. Old relationships seldom die. They take a beating, they crack and crumble, but the pieces are always there begging to be reassembled.

He was a special friend. Deep beneath the weathered exterior was a tender heart, a good guy waiting to happen. I was eager to see him and rebuild our old friendship. My life had a void while he was missing. We had been close friends for thirty years. We grew up together on neighboring farms. We laughed and played and stole watermelons together. We roomed together. Drank together. Ran together. Traveled together. Too bad we never got it together, together.

He had landed in Seattle, miraculously found an honest job, scraped together enough money to rent a modest apartment in an upscale neighborhood, inherited a homeless cat with a history of mental problems, and reported that he rather enjoyed his novel attempt at playing house. At least it was different. And with Bob, different was better.

Several months following our conversation, I was in Seattle for a ministry obligation and purposefully added a couple of play days to my itinerary. Seattle is the most fun city in America, and I seldom pass through it without dedicating some time to sample the wares and revel in the beauty of the ocean and the mountains. I am confident the Lord would count me negligent if I failed to stop and appreciate his artistic and supernatural endeavor in the Great Northwest. Besides, I was afraid Bob would somehow ruin it, too, and I wanted one more look.

Admittedly, it was with some trepidation that I stood on Bob's porch mustering the courage to ring the doorbell. It had been a long time. We had both changed. Our paths and stories had parted company at a distant junction. Was there any common ground left? While fumbling at the door rehearsing my opening lines, Bob intuitively sensed my presence and jerked me inside. Sparing further anxiety, he flashed his trademark grin, hugged my neck, and slipped a mug of Seattle's Best Coffee in my sweaty palm.

He looked different than anticipated. He looked good. Trim and scrubbed, he masked the decades of physical self-abuse that his body had grudgingly endured. He was alert and his eyes beamed with renewal. He had retained his graceful sense of movement, and the cat and I watched with envy as he glided about the apartment. He had cleaned up well.

Nearly twenty years of separation were restored in less than twenty minutes. We had been through too much together to let a little thing like a decade come between us. Within an hour we were wired on coffee and chocolate—the designer drugs of recovering drug addicts— and to negate the buzz he took me down to the Sound for a therapeutic salmon omelet.

I spent the bulk of Saturday afternoon listening to Bob scold his niece about the evils of drugs and casual sex. She was eighteen and had misplaced her brain. Such behavior resided in their genes. She promptly ended the session by graphically instructing amateur counselor Uncle Bob to butt out of her life and let her make her own mistakes—just like he had had the freedom to do. "Freedom," he commented to me after her abrupt departure, "can be a mighty dangerous thing."

Later in the afternoon he persuaded me to accompany him on the daily pilgrimage to his older brother's place. This was no small decision on my part. His brother occupied a crummy little two-room pad on loser-friendly Capital Hill amidst the punks, freaks, homeless misfits, drag queens, lepers, prostitutes, tax gatherers, and other sundry world-class weirdos. It was the untamed west. It was an awful place—an AIDS colony separated from the city by both visible and invisible gates.

Sirens. Trash. Stench. Poverty. Pain. Decay. Darkness. Brokenness. Hopelessness. Death. Satan's calling card was everywhere. This was his turf. Gangs of demons were on every corner sporting his colors, itching for a fight.

"Caution, you who enter here!" screamed the signpost on the edge of this apocalyptic city. "You may come in, and you may even leave, but you will not remain unpolluted from the journey." Well, I'll be go to hell.

I was scared. It wasn't that I was unaccustomed to battling the devil, it was just that I had usually done it on my terms. Evil is much more intimidating when it holds all the cards. I am more comfortable with ministry in a controlled, sterile-air environment.

Bob's brother was dying of AIDS. He got it the old-fashioned way—he earned it. No victim here, instead a committed homosexual.

He was too weak to open the door. We found him huddled in a corner curled up in a semifetal position, valiantly attempting to light another cigarette. The dancing flicker of the match was the only light in the room.

Bob turned on a lamp and his brother's slight shadow was cast on the wall. A 90-pound skeleton doesn't occupy much space. He looked like death. The color of life had departed. He was white as a ghost. For the lucky ones, death is sudden, but for the AIDS candidate, it is a slow, painful, humiliating transition.

As I quickly sized him up, one physical characteristic dominated his appearance. His eyes had grown comparatively large—much like the wolf in Red Riding Hood's grandmother's bed. They were dark and haunting, reminiscent of those seen in photographs of the concentration camps a half-century earlier. I felt like I had invaded a mole's den. I somehow expected to see Gollum appear at any moment with Bilbo Baggins not far behind. This place was a certified nightmare. Here death was not a distant rumor but a stark reality. The Grim Reaper was camped outside, having arrived a few minutes early for his scheduled appointment. I swallowed hard and breathed deep in my valiant effort to keep the vomit down.

I averted my eyes from the zombie's stare and scanned the cave. Bottles and bottles of medicine were stacked carelessly on every horizontal surface, an empty tribute to a man's genius in the face of impending death. Cockroaches had their run of the cell, the only creatures on earth who could delight in such filth. The state-appointed janitor had obviously abandoned his duties months ago, and I silently prayed that I would not catch something penicillin couldn't kill. On the wall by the door hung a cheap plastic frame containing an obnoxious fluorescent bumper sticker: "Life's a Bitch, Then You Die."

We had stopped and bought him some chocolate ice cream. Everybody likes chocolate ice cream. He didn't want any.

In this dungeon, silence was an enemy, so I hummed. "Who's that hummer with you?" he questioned Bob irritably.

"It's our old neighbor, Ron Carlson. Do you remember him?"

There was a twenty-year pause. "Yeah. . . . Yeah, I do remember the little butthead." I was too sick to be offended. "What the hell is he doin' here?" I wondered the same thing.

"He was in town and wanted to stop and see you." Bob lied, but nausea prevented any argument.

"Yeah, I bet he did," Bob's brother chirped sarcastically. He may have been as good as dead, but he had bet right.

"Where are you living, Ron?" He was talking to me.

"Dallas," I meekly responded.

"Dallas! Dallas!!!" He came alive. "That's where I got this damn disease!"

More silence. Another cigarette. Demons partied on the counter.

"Do you go to Father McGee's church?" he asked expectantly before launching into a spirited monologue. "It's called St. Francis. It's up on Walnut Hill. I went there once. Do you know that Father McGee is going to spread my ashes over White Rock Lake in Dallas? Have you ever heard of the legend of the Lady of the Lake? Well, I'm gonna join the bitch and we're gonna terrorize Dallas together!" He seemed pleased by the prospect.

"Consider me presently terrorized." I trembled to myself.

I gave Bob a look that said, "Get me out of here, now!" He ignored me. I spent a week in that room the next hour. I was in worse shape than the dying man. I didn't want any chocolate ice cream either. All I wanted was back to the safety of my rental car and hotel room. But Bob wouldn't let me off that easy. He felt obligated to teach the professional minister something about authentic ministry.

I reluctantly tagged along as he made his rounds through the colony. The tables were turned. I resembled a fish out of water while Bob glided through the muck and mire with graceful ease. He was unhindered by the garbage. Having frequented Hades on earth for thirty years, he was a natural in this dormitory from hell.

He mimicked the Pied Piper. Folks crawled out of their holes to follow him. He touched and hugged and listened. He brought smiles to sullen faces. He provided a spark of energy to this run-down place where batteries needed recharging. The music of his goodness flute filled the hallways with gladness.

Approached by a man too weak to speak, Bob didn't need audible cues to know what he needed. Bob didn't lecture him about the ramifications of same-sex sex; he didn't beat him over the head with a self-righteous club; he didn't kick him when he was down. Instead of shooting the wounded enemy, he gave him a big smile, a pat on the back, and a five-dollar bill. He told me later the man not only had no hope or future, he had no money. "A band-aid for a wound that needs surgery," I protested. "True," he admitted, "but sometimes a band-aid can do wonders for an owie."

Up the stairs, down the corridor, over the river, and through the woods, Bob made his rounds like a well-schooled chaplain. He was a peddler of good cheer, a rejuvenated purveyor of good will. Nobody asked to see his credentials or questioned his seminary training. Degrees aren't worth much in the colony. There is no reason to be pretentious today when there is no tomorrow. Bob provided relief for the moment, and to his flock, that was good enough. They could care less about his sordid background or marginal pedigree. They were solely intent on what he had done for them lately.

The measure of a person's character is often determined by how much good he can wrest from bad. Bob proved to be a man of redemptive character. He had a legion of reasons to cling to failure. His resume was splattered with bad choices and stupid mistakes. The world said he had bad blood. No one gave him much of a chance to make a difference, but he fooled them. He snuck around behind the house and entered ministry through the backdoor. He found a congregation that did church his way.

Ministry has many tracks. Orthodox is good. So is unorthodox. There are conventional ways to do ministry, but there are also unconventional paths. Church sense cuts a side swath. And oftentimes it is the unorthodox and the unconventional that are on the leading edge of compassion. A fine line divides the ragged edge and the cutting edge. The pioneers of new and relevant methods of ministry are often folks with a firsthand knowledge of heartache and trouble. They appear less intimidated by evil and more inclined to roll up their sleeves, hit the streets, and dispense practical kindness. They are more comfortable in the trenches. **They often do good in the name of Jesus without naming names.**

Bob taught me a lot the day we visited hell. He showed me a form of ministry that I did not realize existed. The experience reminded me that anybody, anywhere, any time can leaven life with kindness. He cautioned me about judging the way ministry is practiced. It can be genuine without being textbook.

Impressed with my buddy's grace under fire and obvious potential as a Christian, I invited him to attend church the following morning.

Reluctantly he agreed.

At breakfast he was nervous. "What is wrong?" I asked him.

"What is wrong is the idea of me going to church. I have never been to church, and I am real unsure if I want to start today."

I soothed his fears. Told him how church was just a bunch of regular folks like him and me. No reason to be afraid. Relax. "You'll love it," I assured him.

As we drove in the parking lot that fine summer morning, it was full of Norman Rockwell families, scrubbed and polished, dressed in their Sunday finest, big smiles with oversized white teeth flashing at one another, Bibles under their arms, busily holding doors open for one another. I felt right at home. There is something comforting about dodging brethren in the parking lot.

I turned and gave Bob a big Sunday smile with my oversized white teeth, and he froze. He began to shake. He got the cold sweats. He was in the throws of a panic attack.

I flashed my big Sunday smile to the parking lot brethren and eased the big Rent-a-Buick out onto the frontage road and down the street to the convenience store. Bob stopped shaking and started breathing again.

"What's wrong, pal?" I inquired.

"I can't go in there. I'm not a church guy. I don't look like them. I don't dress like them. I don't smile like them. I ain't got a Bible. I ain't got a chance."

"Whoa," I interrupted. "Take it easy. You overreacted. It's no big deal. They are just regular . . ."

"Whoa," he interrupted. "They may be regular folks, but I'm not!"

Right then, it hit me. Bob was currently experiencing the same emotions that I had felt the day before at the colony. He viewed my brethren the same way I viewed the AIDS-infested homosexuals at the crazy farm! Real church freaked him out. We were the same, only different. Mutually freaked, only by different sets of freaks.

How strange we church folk must appear to the unchurched. Until we become intent on remanufacturing our image into one that is loser-friendly, we will never impact the pagan freaks that fill our cities. Where is our church sense?

The Problem
with Watchdogs

God downloads giant poodles' hard drives with a broad range of software options. Some of the silicone functions better than others. The eating, sleeping, chewing, and mess-making programs are nearly flawless. The fetching, cuddling, and random barking chips are above average. But some programs ought to be kicked back to engineering for redesign. Such is the case with our poodle's "watchdog" software.

Sometime around his inaugural birthday our fuzzy beast decided to reinvent himself by redefining his job description. He requested a transfer to the security division. Our wannabe guard dog envisioned himself as a German Shepherd with a French cut. For weeks he rehearsed his bark until he developed a convincing growl. He harassed the neighborhood felines without mercy. Then one day he read some Jack London stuff we had laying around the house, smiled in the bathroom mirror, and discovered he possessed his own set of white fangs. He was suddenly transformed from campus traffic cop to Special Forces. He grew vigilant. He secured strategic locations to nap—often with one eye open. He slithered. He prowled. He patrolled. He prayed for an unsuspecting intruder.

After several disgusting months of domestic tranquility, our "house dog turned watchdog" grew frustrated with the lack of action. He wanted to bite something. What good are incisors if you can't rip some flesh?

Crime-deprived guard dogs in a secure environment can become dangerously insecure. They lose discernment. Their barking becomes indiscriminate. They bump into things in the night—and bite the thing. They grow paranoid, suspicious, edgy. They smell conspiracy. They snap now and ask questions later. Everything becomes a potential threat and a target. The turf is defended far beyond its need.

Definite bugs in the program. Watchdog virus. Call a troubleshooter.

Any creature with as much pent-up hostility as ours was bound to break sometime. Much to our chagrin, it happened at 3 o'clock in the morning. I was asleep. My wife was asleep. The children were asleep. The bedbugs were asleep. The whole world was asleep. The stupid canine was awake and wired.

Finally, the moment for which he had been preparing arrived.

It started with a subtle series of banging noises in the far corner of the house. Responding to the six-alarm transgression with a ferocious bark, our vigilant pooch ran through the bedroom door and steamed toward the kitchen and the crime scene. Responding to the six-alarm transgression, my wife elbowed me in the ribs and strongly suggested that I get vertical and go investigate the uproar. Raising my head about two inches above the pillow, I screamed at the dog to shut up and go back to sleep. He broke rank and ignored the order.

Now about three-quarters awake. I heard the same noises that had previously sent Deputy Dog into action. They persisted, so I got up, grabbed my bat cane, and stumbled through the house toward the kitchen.

When I arrived, the poodle had his victim trapped in the corner and was growling in a fashion that suggested if he moved an inch he would be minus a foot. The tragic part of the equation for my watchdog was the fact that his victim was nothing more than a bread machine on a wobbly table next to the storage cabinet.

A few days earlier we had bought the new kitchen device so we could have homemade bread like Mom used to make. Sandra had programmed it so that the cycle would begin at 3 a.m. and the finished product would be hot and inviting when we crawled out of the shower at 6 a.m. Nice thought. Poor execution.

When the bread machine went into the knead mode, it shook the little table, which in turn banged against the cabinet sending the patrolling poodle into an uproar. Desperate for action, the dog created an adversary. Zealous to defend the home turf, he stretched his imagination to accommodate his need to patrol. Stupid mutt.

Watchdogs have an upside, but they can also have a downside. They can be valuable critters if legitimate threats lurk in the neighborhood, but always the danger exists that they will create an enemy simply to satisfy their desire to bite something. At times their sense of discernment isn't what it ought to be. That is why I am always a little nervous about the church employing the services of overzealous watchdogs.

The Bible is clear that many legitimate threats face the church. False prophets and crazy doctrines slink around in the shadows waiting for an opportunity to break in and steal something. Joy burglars and hope robbers are constantly trying to sneak in the back door. Various fruits, nuts, and flakes are relentless in their efforts to promote their weird agendas into mainstream thinking.

Threats menace us from without and within. We must be vigilant in protecting the purity of Christ's church, and to do so we need mature and responsible leaders to guard the sacred trust. What we don't need are self-appointed guard poodles masquerading as K-9 units. Many a church and many a fellowship have been seriously injured by zealous but misinformed watchdogs who lack the discernment to determine what really is worth biting. It only makes church sense that they be muzzled and locked in the storeroom where they can't hurt anybody. Sometimes foaming at the mouth can be rabies related.

Too Soon Cool

hat are these?" I asked an upper-classman standing near the washing machine.

"Those are twenty years of unmated socks," he responded. "We keep them in the barrel hoping they will reproduce."

I remember staring in amazement at the thousands of orphaned socks lying unclaimed in the thirty-gallon container. It was 1971, and I was a university freshman lodging in the Kappa Sigma Fraternity House. The laundry room, hidden deep in the bowels of the old building, was a dark and foreboding place. If socks could breed anywhere, they could breed here.

"Whose are they?" I inquired.

"I guess they are anybody's who wants them," he added with a shrug of his shoulders.

He left in a moment and I was all alone with the socks. I adopted twenty of them. Over the course of the next few years, I found a warm and caring home for another hundred. For four years of college I never wore matched socks. I figured that I had two different feet and they deserved to make individual choices. Early on I refused to be intimidated by a little thing like fashion.

Soon afterward, I discovered the local Goodwill store. Bonanza! Bingo! Bonsai! I bought real genuine Hawaiian shirts for two dollars each. This was before they were cool. And they went well with my socks.

For a few dollars a year, I maintained a fine eclectic wardrobe.

Then I graduated, got a job, and had to wear regular stuff. Bummer! Still a little rebellious by nature, I sported irregular underwear.

Turns out I was too soon cool.

Now eclectic is the style.

Fashion designers tell us that the trend of the new millennium will be "fusion," the blending of many styles and cultures highlighted by no recognized formula. Anything and everything goes as wardrobes adopt their own version of "multi-culti." We move to the future with a promise of a more freewheeling approach to the way people dress, a reflection of our increased diversity and varied heritages.

Pop artist Lauryn Hill is promoted as a pioneer of the new fashion statement. Her dress is described as "a little African, a little techno, a little designer, a little thrift, and a little odd." And way cool.

It is going to be a mix and match free-for-all. Hip is gonna' be whatever you want it to be. Pinstripes, polka-dots, and plaids are going to halt their ancient conflict and unite together. Clash is gonna' be cool again! Funky reigns!

I can't wait. Bring me your orphaned socks and your neglected Hawaiian shirts.

Fashion will not be the only dimension of our culture shaped by fusion. Twenty-first century life will be characterized by pluralism, the blending of many minicultures into one maxiculture. The clothes we wear, the food we eat, the books we read, the movies we watch, the homes we build, the information we process, and the gods we serve will all be shaped and selected by a refined process of fusion.

While I celebrate tomorrow's unlimited possibilities and choices in regard to food and clothing, I cringe at what it might do to the Christian faith.

Christianity remains an exclusive religion. It tolerates no competition or compromise. It demands strict allegiance. It leaves no room for trendy alterations in regard to truth and morality. The Bible is clear: one faith, one God, one Savior, one way, one church, one sense.

The challenge confronting us deals with how we handle the inevitable fusion of cultural elements while maintaining a purity of Christian faith. It won't be easy.

Already we see ancient eastern religions and modern New Age practices attempting to join mainstream religious currents. Islam and Hindu adherents are flooding our shores as well as making converts. Subcultures in our large urban areas are quickly constructing hybrid religious expressions. Old heresies are finding common ground in contemporary syncretization. It is more dangerous than cool.

The church must stay straight and narrow no matter the pressures. We must not give in to doctrines or trends that water down the gospel message. We must learn how to attract sinners without accommodating their sin. We must be open to change and new ideas, but we simply cannot compromise the pillars of our faith. We have to welcome differences that don't matter to the Spirit while constantly sifting through the garbage that new believers dump on our porch. It is unthinkable that we would merge our ancient truths with modern half-truths.

Christianity must not become eclectic, because if it does, it is no longer Christianity. Our faith is under no obligation to be cool. Just pure.

Surprised

I'm a little surprised that we permit culture to dictate when and where we shave, when and where we pray.

I'm surprised autocrats aren't taller; more nations aren't deliberately founded on a good idea; anyone would dare mess with Rambo or the I-Hop cashier; people with normal names can't compose classical music; and that cottage cheese could possibly go bad.

I would be real surprised if Mr. Goodwrench doesn't use a bigger hammer; the coyote ever wins; Dolly does her own hair or waist; Alaskans skinny-dip much; or Woody Allen turns out to be a Jedi Knight. Is there any chance that Christopher Columbus or Moses ever asked for directions; Mary Ann could ever go for Gilligan; anyone would want to be reincarnated as Shirley MacLaine; or that any Mexican restaurant really throws out the used hot sauce?

I'm flat-out surprised that even good looking people can't get a decent looking driver's license photo; that her husband brought his golf clubs to the counseling session; that more jerks are not tagged and fitted with shock collars; that cleanliness is right up there with godliness; that they let Forest Gump drive Apollo 13; that Perry Mason won all the cases without ever changing his suit; that my old cat had the nerve to get in the butter dish one last time; that pyramid power can fix a receding hairline; and that God could first love us.

I'm surprised she walks that way.

I'm not surprised that folks like to lodge at Yellowstone Park, Malibu Inn, The East Wing, Petticoat Junction, and the Mansion on Yonder Shore.

I'm surprised we don't have more calluses on our knees.

Don't be surprised when airplanes install vending machines, child ejection seats, Teflon toilet seats, back-up lights, and nose whiskers. Don't be surprised when someday down the road people trust big government, the metric system, the Chinese Zodiac, rookie arbitragers, the preacher count, carnival ride mechanics, and her rendition of life's crooked dealings. Don't be surprised when your local pizza parlor offers its weekly special steamed, sunny-side up, stirred—but not shaken, or tickled pink. Don't be surprised when she grows up and hates Barbie. Don't be surprised when they don't take American Express at the Pearly Gates.

I'm surprised there are not more rehabilitation centers for left-handed scissors operators, pet psychics, clearance sale freaks, adrenaline junkies, chigger breeders, and those who lean on their own understanding.

It is no surprise that lights shine brighter at Christmas.

I'm surprised titans clash, welders waltz, geese gaggle, Nebraska punts, brains freeze, fries french, metaphors mix, and happy hour ain't.

I'm surprised God didn't build more folks with red hair, good judgment, and the luxury option package. I'm not surprised God put the rainbow in the sky.

I'm surprised that a recent inventory check revealed everything I own is broken, out of date, ugly, condemned, expired, illegal, rusted, hungry, or mortgaged.

I'm surprised the Pope shaves on Saturdays; that both you and your dog need Prozac; that your safety engineer thought OSHA was a Japanese cult; that your cousin sold high-tech secrets to the Midianites; that they required proof he picked out the bow tie by himself; that root canals are ever an option; that Arkansaw is spelled wrong; that this restaurant is not under new management; and that it is not a felony to apply make-up in morning traffic.

I'm not surprised dogs, newlyweds, and candy makers drool.

I'm not surprised to learn that he recently fell off the turnip truck or crashed in dirty underwear. I'm not surprised *these* tickets or *this* popcorn were discounted. I'm not surprised that wise men still seek Him!

Don't be surprised when God gets the last word.

I'm surprised how good Betty Crocker looks at seventy-five, the preacher sounds from the back pew, fake crab looks in the deli section, and Charlie Brown's team looks in March.

It is surprising that some folks think they can tell who is and who ain't!

Don't act surprised when she burns the lima beans on purpose, cancels your permit, shortens your shelf life, finds a new model that is voice activated, and suggests you spend more time howling and less time dozing.

Don't act so surprised when your guardian angel tugs.

I'm not a bit surprised that they traded Manhattan for a bag of trinkets; bat manure miners and baby-sitters are rich; dust bunnies multiply; husband number nine feels a little inadequate; "self-help" books are big sellers; high school principals have a mean streak; vacation spots cheat tourists and drunks; He keeps track of who's been naughty and who's been nice; tobasco sauce enhances road kill; he did this remodeling all by himself; and children and sausage are made in private.

I'd be surprised if all religions lead to the one God.

Don't act surprised when your child announces that she has changed her college major to line dancing—and it's a six-year program; that she has taken a job as a lightning bug researcher and part-time storm chaser; that she and her new husband plan to breed emus and Volkswagens for fun and profit; that she is uncontrollably governed by bizarre biological binges; that she has no back-up plan; that she has been drinking straight from the carton for fifteen years; and that she resents her father for blowing his nose with his fingers!

The church was surprised when their preacher returned from the holy lands with an actual skeleton of the baby Moses.

I'd be surprised if God let you become too comfortable, too sassy, or too self-reliant.

Don't be surprised when "day-old" is an understatement, the rebate offer excludes American citizens; Ralph Nader starts driving a used Yugo; you learn his parents were first cousins; mink and beauty queens dismiss their caretakers; your neighborhood Animal Hospital offers you a "loaner dog"; your new analgesic does not double as a hemorrhoid medicine; and you can't get a good chicken fried steak medium rare.

I am surprised our highly technological culture continues to underestimate the effectiveness of the: burp, blink, chill, sneeze, scratch, stretch, shiver.

I am not surprised my neighbor built a fence; my boss is a bowling league president; the weatherman got his Ph.D. from a matchbook cover; normal people covet the handicap sticker; and that your camouflage fooled neither the deer nor your wife!

I'm surprised we don't try a little harder to act like the One who made us!

I'm surprised supermodels are burdened with bathroom stops; more working people don't stay at the Holiday Inn; metro drivers think "merge right" is a Republican campaign slogan; chihuahuas and punks are so concerned with territorial rights; and Moroni found the golden plates instead of the golden fleece.

I'm surprised she pushed over the Port-a-potty—especially with him in it!

We are going to be surprised when we find out who the really blessed people turn out to be!

I'm surprised we don't have better church sense.

It should come as no surprise that bears do their business in the woods; big dogs leave the porch; some species eat their young; the rich and famous do things differently; Shakespeare flunked English 101—three times; and that some days you can't keep up with losers!

Don't be surprised when chocolate is officially designated the sixth food group; trash tabloids get sued by the Loch Ness monster's agent; the duckbilled platypus mounts a public relations campaign; and modern science explains the purpose of the thingamajig that hangs down the back of your throat.

Don't be surprised when the devil shows up in his Sunday best or starts running infomercials on Saturday night television.

Don't be surprised if Jesus comes knocking again.

Don't be surprised when Christ's church goes home early.

Minivan Banter

Want to go crazy in two weeks?
Want to ruin a perfectly good summer?
Want to peddle your children to the next marauding minivan caravan?
Then plan a family vacation today!

Vacationing with young children is a great idea—in theory. In reality it is certifiable insanity. Healthy and whole family units stay that way by shunning extended time together in close quarters. Families that stay together don't vacation in a car together. Family value structures are seldom enhanced by massive doses of minivan banter.

The single poorest summer decision mom and dad can make is to load three young children in an automobile and head out on a three-day journey into the wilderness. It is impossible to come away unscathed. They will return, at best, damaged goods. When Jesus invited the little children to come unto him, he was not planning on taking them to Jericho for spring break.

Kids are great on vacation—for the first hour. Then it is nonstop damage control. They get restless. They get bored. They get ornery. They substitute confrontation for tranquility. They fight to pass the time. Inexperienced parents leave for vacation as idealists; they return as battered realists. Big folks think that all passengers drive cross-country to see the sights and enjoy America. Children believe it is a time to plan WWIII.

Children on vacation are quick to exercise their creative genius juices. Even though the adult population has carefully organized every detail of the trip, young ones fabricate issues over which to whine and fight. Adults think that their behavior is childish, forgetting that their children are poster children for childish behavior. Research has indicated that 96% of children on vacation spend the majority of their time fighting with their siblings. The other 4% are comatose.

There is no end of matters over which children can bicker. The other one always has more than his share. Competition for the premier sitting place in the backseat is usually intense. It is worth noting that the best seats change, depending on where big sister sits. Nothing like a little border dispute to keep the natives on edge. Initiating discussion on where the next meal will occur is a monumental mistake. The blame game is also a family favorite. A late afternoon winner is a guessing game about which little ankle-biter can produce the strangest noise or smell. Since there is no objective standard to gauge the performance, controversy can continue into the evening hours. If all else fails, they can always argue about the color of the highway, the length of the Pope's beard, or how many angels can dance on the head of a pin.

Parents need the wisdom of Solomon to referee the endless squabbles generated by displaced children. It seems impossible for mere mortals to determine who touched whom first and who chose first last.

Vacations are scripted to be fun. They are usually ruined by controversy and unresolved conflict. Enduring two weeks of bickering and grumbling makes any parent grateful to get back to work and rest in peace.

Vacations share similar patterns with the way we sometimes do church. Church is scripted to be fun, but oftentimes it is ruined by endless controversy and unresolved conflict. Occasionally church folks behave like children bored in the backseat of a minivan. Too often our faith community is characterized by a spirit of controversy that quenches the unity of the Holy Spirit.

What makes children, and some adults, so disagreeable? Why do good Christian folks spend so much time and energy arguing about matters that don't warrant their attention? What is it about religious stuff that breeds conflict? How is it that born-again believers frequently get bogged down squabbling about things that are incidental, usually emotionally supercharged, and often unsolvable? Why do we go looking for a fight? Why do we defy good church sense?

The questions surrounding dancing angels, endless genealogies, and communion cups are never going to be solved to everyone's satisfaction. So leave them alone and move on to the important stuff. Don't allow marginal issues to distract you from pursuing wisdom from above. If you spend too much time worrying about who touched whom first, you may miss God's touch.

Blessed are the peacemakers. Cursed are the division makers.

Obviously a constant diet of important matters demand our energies. There are issues over which good people disagree, but even then it must be done in an agreeable fashion. Mature folks must constantly determine what is important and what is mere sectarian trash talk. There will always be some knucklehead baiting you into a controversy trap. Don't be a sucker. Don't let a spoiled child drag you down to his level. You can never win a squirting contest with a skunk. You can never win a conflict with a troublemaker who thrives on controversy, unless of course, you're the devil.

Living on the Ragged Edge

Television networks, desperate to survive in an era of increasing competition and reduced market share, scramble every fall to produce hit shows that might attract new viewers, particularly viewers who will buy the stuff their advertisers have to sell, themselves trying to survive in an era of increased competition and reduced market share. They all eat from the same trough.

It remains unclear if pop culture shapes television or if television shapes pop culture, but neither one of them has much to crow about. Every year the new shows get trashier. Columnist John Leo says that producers of contemporary television are bottom feeders generating "smut-see TV." At the very least, they are doing more than their share to dumb down culture.

How much juvenile bathroom humor can we stand? At what point do we finally get totally grossed-out? How much teen angst can nonteens handle? How stupid can stupid be before we reclaim moral sanity?

In today's senseless marketplace, television has to be edgy or it fails. It seems that audiences are tired of the same old standard fare. They desire new and wild stuff. Viewers expect to be turned on, hyped up, jacked around, ticked off, and grossed out. Shock value is the key ingredient to success. New shows have to prom-

ise to go where no show has gone before or remote-happy viewers will switch to the Simpson's, where shock value and irrever-
ence have been standard fare for a decade. A new program must
incorporate a sharp edge that slices and dices traditional norms or
it will be considered dull, irrelevant, and worse yet—decent.
Decency is the kiss of death in the entertainment industry.
Entertainment has come a long way—most of it downhill.

I don't watch much TV, but I recently stumbled on the pilot
program for one of the networks' hot new fall samplings. I decided to give it a look. Bad decision.

It was a hospital show, a drama, I think. Perhaps a comedy
with lots of tragedy. On second thought, I'm inclined to label it
under the horror category.

The story jumped from subplot to subplot, from dysfunctional character to dysfunctional character. Each wing of the
urban hospital had a mini-drama in the works.

On the east wing, a seven year old boy was diagnosed with a
bizarre life-threatening disease. The staff surgeon refused to do
the required surgery because he had killed the last child with a
similar diagnosis. There was a new doctor on staff who was eager
to operate, but she had curly hair and cleavage, and the other doctors didn't like her. The kid's parents were incompetent fools who
couldn't make a decision.

The west wing had worse problems. A middle-aged man had
just died on the operating table during a simple liposuction surgery because a distracted surgeon had forgotten about him.
Honest mistake, he claimed. The surviving spouse secured a
rough-and-tumble attorney who wanted the whole west wing as
ransom. I learned more about liposuction than I ever wanted to
know. I'll keep my spare tire, thank you.

Over on the north wing, a Catholic priest was in emergency
surgery having his penis reattached. It had been bitten off by: **a)**
a robber (if you believe the priest), **b)** a prostitute (if you believe
the hospital doctor who was part of his parish).

On the south wing Bart Simpson was getting a lobotomy, his
little sister serving as guest surgeon.

I lasted about twenty-five minutes. And I won't be back.

It was rude, crude, and lewd. It was in-your-face dysfunctionality. Jerry Springer would have been proud. It was enough to make me throw up.

The networks call it edgy.

What they fail to tell us sad sack viewers is that it is on the ragged moral edge.

What is it that attracts us to the ragged edge, that precarious little chunk of turf steadily crumbling apart and tumbling into the canyon below? Is it the thrill? The adrenaline rush? The danger? The devil? It sure ain't good sense.

Perhaps an illustration will help clarify our very present danger. While visiting Mt. Rainier State Park several years ago, we stopped at the highest scenic viewpoint to take some pictures. An awesome and inspiring panorama of glaciers and mountain peaks, the vantage point was a magnet for tourists. To arrive at this point, we had climbed 5000 feet from the valley below. Mt. Rainier loomed another 10,000 feet nearly straight up. In a word: majestic.

The scenic stop was full of cars, people, and cameras. All but two were well-behaved (people, that is, all the cars and cameras were in order).

For five minutes I listened to a beleaguered set of parents lecture their rambunctious 5-year-olds at least five times about the danger of straying past the five-foot tall protective railing. The advice went in one ear and raced out the other.

We tourists simultaneously jumped five feet in the air when the mother screamed. Her thrill-seeking little missiles had scaled the barricades and were precariously perched on the ragged edge of the cliff, a few inches from a shear 5000' drop-off into the raging river below.

They were oblivious to the danger. In fact, they reveled in the instant attention.

Dad successfully coaxed them back to solid ground, and we moved on without further incident, but it was a close call, and we all agreed that the next time they might not be so lucky.

It is as if we have devolved into a culture of out-of-control five-year-olds intent on crossing protective railings to secure a front row seat on the ragged edge.

What do we do for our next big thrill? Replace the fluoride in our water with cocaine? Sponsor Saturday night orgies at the city park? Bring back the gladiators and the lions? Murder Beaver Cleaver on the operating table? If we surrender common moral sense to impulse and appetite, where does it end?

It ends when the cliff gives way. Prime-time television, postmodern rejection of objective truth, dark and violent music, national endorsement of the murder of unborn children, and a long list of moral diseases suggest that the turf is crumbling below our feet.

It is the church that must coax culture back to safe and solid ground. The ragged edge is ground suited only for the nimble feet of the devil. Nothing good happens out there.

Last at Bat
before the Lord Comes

I n the "dog days" of August, 1939, the conversation of the average American male was focused on the developing careers of two dynamic individuals. The primary topic of discussion was the leader and master orator behind the swelling popularity of Germany's Third Reich, Adolph Hitler. His venomous rhetoric, seasoned with hatred and bigotry, was a growing menace to world peace and stability. America had one eye riveted on the threatening events transpiring on the other side of the Atlantic, while the other eye twinkled at the possibilities of a rising super-star.

Ted Williams was the most widely heralded young ball player to enter the Major Leagues in decades. He was nineteen years young, still wet behind the ears, but his mighty lumber was screaming for attention, and the Boston Red Sox could delay his immigration to the Big Leagues no longer. He had batted .388 in the Minor Leagues, and his reputation as a slugger generated headlines on sports sections of newspapers across the land. He was good—real good! Many scouts, both professional and of the coffee shop variety, believed he was the next Roy Hobbs.

Teddy Baseball played his first Major League game in the blinding spotlight of America's premier baseball city. As he stepped to the plate for the first time, his ears rang with the screaming delight and ruthless jeers of those who zealously occupied "the house that Ruth built"—legendary Yankee Stadium. In the circus-like atmosphere of the Bronx, his past accomplishments meant nothing; this was center stage in the Big Tent, and Yankee fans stood unimpressed with a rookie, especially one from Beantown.

The rookie was baptized into the real world of American League pitching by future Hall-of-Famer Red Ruffing, a crafty veteran of many a battle. The Yankee hurler baffled Williams with an assortment of pitches and at evening's end Ted the Great was 0 for 5. The next day brought Williams little more success as recently acquired Spud Chandler duplicated Ruffing's performance. The rookie left the park a beaten man. According to Curt Gowdy, collector of baseball lore, Williams showered quickly that afternoon and returned to his room at the Roosevelt Hotel. Confused and humiliated, he skipped dinner with his teammates and locked himself in his room. He lay on his bed, the darkened and sullen space a stark contrast to his experience a few hours earlier at the stadium, and wondered what went wrong. His anxiety quickly turned to tears, and as he wept on his pillow he asked himself over and over again: "What's wrong with me?"

He knew he could hit. He knew that he was better than he had demonstrated the prior two days. He knew he belonged in the Show. But what was wrong? As he labored over the depressing events of the last two games, the answer to his dilemma suddenly hit him like a Bob Feller fastball! The problem was his concentration! The bright lights, screaming fans, newspaper hype, and ghosts of hallowed Yankee Stadium had distracted him. He had lost his focus, and it had cost him dearly.

He quickly formulated a remedy that would benefit him the rest of his career. As he stood in the batter's box for his first at-bat in the final game of the three-game series with the Yankees, he paused for just a moment and lectured himself: "Ted Williams, this is the last bat you'll ever have in the Big Leagues, so you had better make it count!" It became the cornerstone of his hitting routine. From that moment on, every time he stepped to the plate, he repeated the motivating phrase that helped make him the finest ballplayer to ever grace America's game. "Ted Williams, this is your final at bat—make it count."

This is the type of concentrated commitment that we need to demonstrate as Kingdomites. This is the level at which we must focus if we hope to live successful and abundant Christian lives. We need to view every at-bat as our last at-bat.

We need to live everyday as if "this is my last day on earth, and I must make it count!" We would be wise if we approached every relationship with the attitude that "this is my last opportunity to show my love for this person!" We might convert the world if we adopted the mentality that "this is the last chance I will have to share the gospel with this person!" The church would flourish if we approached it with the zealous commitment that "this is my last chance to sacrifice myself for the glory of God and his precious bride!" Heaven will be full of God's people if we live everyday like "this is our last at-bat before the Lord comes again!"

In a distracting and antagonistic world, we must stay focused on that which is important. Keep your eyes upon Jesus, the Author and Perfecter of your faith! And lay off the curve ball in the dirt.

It Looks Bad!

Let's call him Norman. If his true identity was revealed, it could damage his reputation. People would think he is weird.

Norman got sick. He didn't mean to. He didn't want to. For a long time he even pretended it wasn't so.

Finally Norman had to go to his doctor. The doctor asked what was wrong and when Norman told him, the doctor said, "That's weird." Norman told him some more weird stuff and the doctor shook his head in disbelief. It didn't make sense. He told Norman to take two aspirin and if he wasn't better to call him in the morning. He wasn't better.

Norman's doctor told him it sounded like stress, but he referred him to an ear, nose, and throat specialist just in case a bug was on the loose. Mr. ENTerprise poked and jabbed Norman for an hour. He charged him $400 and told him he was dehydrated. "Quit drinking so much coffee and stop that fake coughing." Norman felt guilty about his caffeine habit and apologized to the receptionist. Maybe it was guilt and not stress.

Then he got a fever.

"It looks bad," said his doctor.

"What is it?" Norman asked.

"I don't have the faintest idea," said his doctor, "but it is bad."

"What do I do?" Norman inquired.

"You need to see a pulmonologist."

Norman went to the pulmonologist six times. Had his blood taken eight times. Six different X-rays. "Looks like a weird fungal infection," the pulmonologist said. The doctor ran a long thinga-magig down Norman's throat and into his lungs. No fungus. No bugs. No answers. "Got to be an infection somewhere else," the lung doctor declared.

Norman was hustled upstairs to an infectious disease special-ist. "Ah, hah," she said. "Hepatitis A, B, or C!" Norman felt like it was "D"—all of the above.

"Is that bad?" Norman inquired.

"Could be," she said.

All the tests came back negative.

"Must be AIDS," she comforted Norman. "Do you have insurance?"

Norman bolted for the door, bottles of medicine falling from his pockets.

"Come back," she screamed, "there are still a few antibiotics we haven't tried!"

"Let's visit an orthopedic surgeon," Norman's family doctor suggested. "Perhaps you have an infection in a joint. Maybe staph, or stiff, or weird stuff."

The orthopedist referred Norman to a dermatologist (they were brothers-in-law). Norman went as commanded, but when the dermatologist asked why he had come, Norman couldn't remember.

"Looks like allergies," the doctor said. "Stay away from air-ports, zoos, and poison oak. Rub this on the places that hurt and don't pick your nose."

Norman got worse by the week. His big toe began to throb. He visited the neighborhood podiatrist. "Did you stub it?" he asked.

"No, Sir," Norman answered.

"That's weird," the doctor replied. "Most everybody I see has stubbed their toe."

"Not me," said Norman confidently.

"I'll bet you did, and you can't remember it," the doctor argued.

"Any idea why my toes, my lungs, and my head all hurt at the same time?" Norman hesitantly inquired.

"Your shoes are too tight!"

Norman surrendered his co-pay and headed back to his primary care physician.

"Beats me," said Norman's doctor. "Want to see a rheumatologist for fun?"

"This ain't fun anymore," Norman told his doctor. "I'd give anything for an accurate diagnosis."

"You have Still's Disease," said the rheumatologist, "it's real weird!"

"What can I do?" asked Norman.

"Learn to live with it and quit going to other doctors."

"I can live with that," said Norman.

The lesson to this story is that if you are going to get sick, then get something that your primary care physician can diagnose and treat. Don't get something weird.

It seems that modern medicine, with all its technological advancements, is often characterized by the poke-and-hope diagnostic method. If a patient ever gets a series of irregular symptoms, then a corresponding series of misdiagnoses inevitably follow.

A similar problem exists in the spiritual/mental/emotional health community as legions of experts work diligently to misdiagnose sin. Secular technicians tell broken and hurting people that their symptoms are a product of environmental pollution, bad parents, high taxes, poor schools, junk food, second-hand smoke, El Nino, tight shoes, and Urban Sprawl. It doesn't make sense. Truth is: Sin!

Church is a hospital for sinners. We need to treat as many as possible, as quickly as possible. It will save a lot of frustration.

I Can't Keep It Inside

I love alcoholics who don't drink anymore. I am particularly fond of recovering alcoholics who at one time had completely and absolutely bottomed out. I love to listen to the testimony of folks who had their lives absolutely and completely destroyed by alcohol. Now they have a story to tell.

Successful recovering alcoholics are fully committed to sobriety; those who aren't, aren't. They believe, or they fail.

Sobriety is more about attitude than physical chemistry. Alcoholics must first prevail between their ears before they can win the battle with the bottle. Alcoholics Anonymous preaches that a drunk can only overcome the enemy if the mind is first transformed by Divine power. Only God (as you define Him to be) can regenerate a reprobate heart. Only God can provide the power to believe, the strength to endure.

For those who grasp the formula and surrender to Divine power, the hope of sobriety becomes a reality. Then the real problems begin. It is much harder to stay sober than get sober. Most alcoholics have quit drinking a hundred times; it ain't hard to quit. The only measure of success that matters for an alcoholic is sustained sobriety. And sustained sobriety depends on an attitude that believes addiction can be overcome.

Back to why I love recovering alcoholics. Somewhere along their journey, they discovered that the best way to stay sober is to tell others about the benefits of living straight. Successful longtime recovering alcoholics actively involve themselves in the struggles of other recovering addicts. In doing so, they reinforce their own commitment. By sharing their beliefs they not only assist other struggling pilgrims, but they strengthen their own resolve as well. It is part of the conversion dynamic. From drunk to sober is a million mile journey, and the only way to get there is to construct a shared belief system.

While serving as a missionary in the mountains of British Columbia during the early 1980s, we encountered one of the world's most interesting characters. Art Krane was a 55-year-old woodsman born and raised in the Canadian Rockies: part Grizzly Adams, part Mother Teresa, and part John the Baptist. A cougar hunting legend, he had given up the sport because he felt like it was unchristian to train his hounds with the neighbors' house cats. Understand that he had been converted.

A drunk for nearly forty years, he had come to the idea of God through Alcoholics Anonymous and to Jesus through a missionary that preceded us. Zealous was his middle name. He was turned on by freedom—freedom from strong spirits, freedom in the Spirit. And he wanted the whole world to be free.

Art nearly wore me out in those brief two years we spent in Canada. He dragged me to meeting after meeting, Bible study after Bible study, ministry after ministry. A relentless warrior for Jesus, many people scattered when they saw him approaching. I just tried to keep up.

One snowy night on the way home from a fruitless Bible study with an old hermit deep in the woods, I asked him: "Art, why do you keep up this frantic pace?"

He stared straight ahead and didn't speak for several moments. Then a sly smile crept across his face and he submitted an answer I'll never forget: "Because I can't help it," he said. "I'm sober; I'm saved; I just have to tell others. I can't keep it to myself."

At that moment, I received insight into the nature of conversion that I had not previously considered. **People who evangel-**

ize don't do it because they have to, but because they have to! They cannot help it. They are so turned on with Jesus that they can't keep the Good News bottled up inside their hearts. They simply have to share it.

Art apologized for being a simple man (in fact he was one of the most complex men I have ever known), and continued: "Let me tell you something I learned in AA. The only way I can stay sober is to help others stay sober. And now I have learned that the only way I can stay saved is to help others get saved." Made good church sense to me.

Sharing your faith begins with an appreciation for salvation. Do you shy away from helping others receive salvation? Then take a close look at your own salvation. How important is it to you? Are you consumed with God's daily grace? Do you appreciate the fact that the Father sent his Son to the cruel cross of Calvary for your sin? Do you realize that God has made a way for you—at terrible cost? Do you know your Savior? Are you impressed?

Christian, convert thyself!

Flow, River, Flow

The Fairmont Hot Springs Resort, nestled in the Rocky Mountains of fabulous eastern British Columbia, boasts one of the world's most beautiful golf courses. Teeing off on the monstrous 660-yard, par-five third hole, the dazed golfer gazes out over the headwaters of the Columbia River. A small plaque makes note of the geographical significance. The distraction serves as a good excuse for a triple bogey. (It took me three fairway woods to see the green!)

Standing on a naked bluff outside Portland, Oregon with a stiff, cool breeze rumbling down the gorge, a mere human is overwhelmed with the magnitude of the Columbia River. Still a hundred miles from the Pacific Ocean and Cape Disappointment, the great river is a mile wide and deeper than your imagination. A lot of water has to come together to make it happen.

The Snake River begins as a trickling stream in the shadow of Wyoming's majestic Teton Mountains near Jackson Hole. It rambles and rolls across southern Idaho, turns north at Boise, roars through America's deepest gorge—the famed white waters of Hell's Canyon, and then cruises into Lewistown, Idaho, where it converges with the Clearwater River.

The Clearwater has its origins in the Bitteroot Mountains

along the Idaho-Montana border just west of the Continental Divide. Fed by annual snow packs of more than a hundred inches, the crystal clear waters of the west's most uncivilized drainage join forces along the trail hiked by Lewis and Clark at the beginning of the 19th century. It willingly mates with the Snake, and the two gain speed for their rendezvous with the Columbia at Pasco, Washington.

The legendary "River of No Return" is actually the Salmon, a raging and violent river that calls the Sawtooth Mountains of primitive central Idaho its home. It graciously awaits the Snake's departure from Hell's Canyon and then gently merges its spent waters with those of its ancient kin.

A couple miles downstream from Paradise, Montana, the Flathead River converges with the Thompson River, and the waters of the Purcell Mountains become one with those of the Whitefish and Flathead Ranges, little sisters in the vast Rocky Mountain chain. Flowing in and out of the lakes of northern Idaho, these rivers join the Kootenai, the Clark Fork, the St. Joe, the Coeur d'Alene, the Spokane, and others. At some point they all find their way to the mighty Columbia. And they all finally make it home, the vast Pacific making room for all its children.

One doesn't have to be a nature freak to be impressed with God's handiwork in the great Northwest. And nowhere are the marvels of God better displayed than in his transportation of the mountain shower to the distant ocean. "All the rivers flow into the sea, yet the sea is not full. To the place where the rivers flow, there they flow again" (Ecclesiastes 1:7).

Most interesting about the network of rivers that comprise the Columbia are their points of convergence. They meet. They greet. They agree. They advance together. They become one. United. Indivisible. Harmonious.

The more I contemplate the workings of the Columbia River, the more I see the workings of the church. Her personality is highlighted by an endless series of convergences.

Much is made today about convergence, the new buzzword of technology and business. Folks are hip on converging various technologies, industries, utilities, cultural entities, and distinct worldviews. It makes for some weird pairings. Fact and fiction now run together. As do right and wrong. Same goes for good and evil, black and white, night and day. Bible publishers are owned by secular giants and your neighborhood funeral home isn't family-owned anymore. Washington has gone to Hollywood and Hollywood has merged with crazy. Country is cool in the city and city is craved in the country. Strange bedfellows are the norm.

I remain skeptical that mixing everything together is always in anything's best interest. No matter what paint colors you mix together, it always comes out drab gray. There is a place for convergence and a place for individuality, and our culture must learn to distinguish the difference. It requires good church sense.

The church is a mighty river comprised of a million streams, a zillion droplets united together by a common goal, a mighty force on a journey home.

We are God's handiwork: created by him, guided by him, protected by him, inspired by him, kept by him. Our journey is marked by constant convergence with his other forces, his other children. Our role is to meet, to greet, to agree, to advance together, to become one.

Come, join the river, before you evaporate all alone.

Don't Flush That Reptile!

T he story began with great promise. It also boasted an impeccable source. My friend said she had read it somewhere. Fascinated by the possibilities, I did a little Internet research into Eskimo linguistics. I needed to make sure that Nanook of the North really had two hundred different words for "snow." That is a lot of fine white powder.

I wanted the factoid to be true. It would be great material for illustration purposes. *"Just as the Eskimos have hundreds of different words for snow, so Christians have multiple ways to describe the beauty of church fellowship."* I figured if primitive Eskimos could develop a snow-sophisticated language, then Christians could do the same with church lingo.

Nice try. Unfortunately, it is not true. In reality, Eskimos have three or four words for snow that are comparable to our "blizzard" and "sleet." It turns out the story is well circulated but not well documented. It is just another urban legend.

Urban legends are modern day kissing cousins to yesterday's vintage folklore. Rather than stories from the old west of Pecos Bill and Paul Bunyan, today's myths deal with albino alligators occupying New York sewers and organ pirates breaking into a Las Vegas hotel room and robbing a man's kidneys. Or perhaps you have heard the story about Proctor and Gamble promoting Satan worship with a cryptic astrological trademark on their products. Maybe you have talked to someone whose first cousin's best friend found a field mouse in his soda bottle or a deep-fried rat in her nachos. I still get letters warning about Madelyn O'Hare's efforts to legislate paganism and wipe out Christianity. My secretary had an e-mail the other day warning about AIDS-infected syringes being hidden in theater seats. The world is terrorizing enough without fictional gore!

Urban legends are simply a part of culture that reflects our fears and anxieties. From Sasquatches to spy watches, bogeymen remain alive and well in our brain's inner recesses.

One of the characteristics of an urban myth is its capacity for exaggeration. Each time it is shared, the story is enhanced and its shock value increased. Even more incredible is the fact that as people share the myth, they often take ownership, casting aside reason and credibility in favor of cosmic dysfunctionality. Folks just want to believe the bizarre. We like tales stranger than life. We embrace nonsense.

Two thousand years ago the church of Jesus Christ was founded on the most bizarre event in human history. A man claiming to be the incarnate Son of God came to earth, born of a virgin woman. After a brief spell of miraculous activity and radical preaching, he was executed on a cross outside Jerusalem, the holy city of the Jews. There he died. He was buried in a rock tomb nearby. Three days following his death, visitors to the gravesite found the tomb empty. This man had fulfilled his own prophecy—he had risen from the dead! Fact and fiction would never be the same. Nonsense became church sense. Fear, anxiety, and despair have been replaced by hope and promise.

Jesus Christ was resurrected from the dead. God broke into the world and reversed the cycle of sin and death.

Two millennia later, the story is the same. It differs from urban folklore in that it is true and requires no exaggeration. How can this story be enhanced? It is a universal reality.

The church is the living product of the resurrection. The story of God's love as demonstrated in the life, death, and resurrected life of Jesus is the power of salvation. We possess the greatest story ever told. It is the life-giving, life-changing, lifeblood of our very existence. And scripture promises that "all the bogeymen of hell shall not prevail against it" (Matthew 16:18).

Ya' Gotta Believe!

For nearly a decade, the hapless New York Mets were the laughingstock of professional baseball. They lost games in ways never imagined, often defying both logic and tradition. Casey Stengel, their colorful manager, once suggested that his woeful lot of misfits had revolutionized the fine art of defeat.

Then came the "Amazing Mets" of 1969, a season fondly remembered in baseball lore. The transformed Mets shocked the world and won the World Series! Nobody believed they could do it—nobody but themselves.

By mid-season the born-again "Miracle Mets," New York's other team, adopted the slogan that propelled them to the pinnacle of sports fame: "Ya' Gotta' Believe!"

And believe they did! Remarkably their belief translated into improved play on the field. They stopped dropping pop-ups. They hit the cut-off man. They got the bunt down. They waited on the curve ball and hit it to right field. They stopped beating themselves. They learned how to win.

The Mets were transformed in their minds before they were reinvented on the field. Their heroics began with a new attitude and a new perspective. They first had to whip the doubts that plagued them between the ears before they could whip the demons that haunted them between the foul lines.

Every great project begins with a committed and enthusiastic attitude that says: "I believe!"

Consider the events of our own brief history. The hapless pilgrims survived the harsh odds of a new land because they first believed in their mission of freedom. America prevailed in the revolutionary war because the power of the cause was stronger than British artillery. The industrial revolution transformed America and the world because the nation first believed it could accomplish great things. The good guys won the great wars because we first won the battle of the minds. We have defeated communism and taken our place as the world's only superpower primarily because of an indomitable attitude. We prevail in deed because we first prevail in thought. We become what we think. There is unlimited power in the will to achieve. Never underestimate a people with a cause bigger than themselves. Never discount the role that attitude plays in regard to conquest.

With this principle in mind, it becomes obvious that Christian evangelism and church mission are inseparably linked to the disciple's belief quotient. How else can one explain the first-century Christian explosion? The early Christians believed the gospel, and their commitment to the reality of Christ's resurrection transformed them into Spirited evangelists. Whether it is the first century or the twenty-first century, where believers are intensely enthusiastic about their faith, evangelism will naturally erupt. The Spirit will blow mightily.

Evangelism is first and foremost an attitude, the product of a heart set on fire by God's grace, the result of a positive relationship between you and God, the manifestation of God's love working in you. Evangelism is spontaneous combustion, energy that can't stay still.

Powerful evangelism begins in your heart and in your head. The best programs can't compensate for a lack of enthusiasm or devotion. If you don't first believe it, if you are not first turned on by it, if you are not first overwhelmed by it, then you have little chance to convince others to believe it. **Converting others begins with your own authentic conversion.**

Christians, "Ya' gotta believe!"

Church sense will not prevail in the third millennium because of superior programs or facilities. The Kingdom will only come when Kingdomites first win the battle of the mind. The transformation of the mind can only come from an intimate relationship with Jesus. When you really know Jesus, you'll find a way to ensure that others know, too.

Who Lowered the Bar?

What do brussels sprouts, panda bears, purple shoes, Russian last names, Edsels, two-strike bunts, and Matthew 7:1 have in common?

They are all misunderstood.

Is there another scripture in all of Holy Writ that suffers the same abuse and misuse as these words from Jesus' teaching on the Mount?

Who duped us into believing that this passage prohibits Christians from calling sin a sin and admonishing brethren to stop sinning, clean up their act, and get it right?

Has our culture of tolerance and hypernonjudgmentalism so influenced our thinking that we are willing to allow self-centered spiritual rebels to dictate our exegesis and force us to surrender biblical authority?

When did we lower the bar? When did the relative righteousness—or better, lack of righteousness—of our do-your-own-thing-without-consequences-lifestyle become the Christian's worldview? Why have we allowed secular thinking to pollute the way we interpret Scripture and work out our faith within the community of believers? When did we lose our mind? When did we abandon church sense?

A case, or two, in point.

My wife and I listened patiently as a longtime Christian preacher and his wife explained the recent plight of their son. After fifteen years of marriage, their daughter-in-law had become dissatisfied with their son's sexual contribution to the union, and to remedy the conjugal dilemma, she had taken a lover and moved him into the guest bedroom. He was at her disposal and serviced her needs on demand.

With predictable sensitivity I responded to the stranger-than-fiction tale: "Is that right?" I really wanted to say, "Is that so?" They concluded their explanation by assuring us that all four members of the equation (there was also a 14-year-old grandson in the mix) had adapted well and were communing as one big happy family. In fact, they said, their son was relieved that someone else was servicing the account. The pressure was off.

Seldom dumbfounded, I picked myself up off the floor, a result of passing out and tumbling from my seat. "Are you really okay with this situation?" I carefully inquired.

"Well, we are learning to live with it," they responded simultaneously. "And we want our kids to be happy."

"Doesn't it seem a little out of Christian character?" I asked, while defending my ribs from Sandra's pointed elbow. "Doesn't the Bible condemn this sort of adulterous affair?"

It was as if I had taken a can of red spray paint and marked their chests with a giant A. They looked at me like I was a graffiti pervert. They leaned forward in their chairs, and with a stern glare the old preacher raised his voice and scolded us: "The Bible says, 'Judge not, lest you be judged.'"

Conversation postponed due to lack of reason.

As President William Jefferson Clinton's troubles with a young intern began to unfold during the summer of 1998, heated exchanges between partisan camps became the norm. Conservative Christians stared in amazement at the purported results from national polls (Have you ever been polled? Do you know anyone who has ever been polled?) indicating that his presidential approval rating actually rose during the conflict. The message was clear: "As long as the economy is strong, we don't care what kind of hanky-panky goes on in the White House. It's Hillary's problem, not ours, and who are we to judge their private relationship?"

Through the course of the debate, I marveled at the number of times folks who hadn't turned to the Bible for instruction in years—if ever—were quoting Matthew 7:1 to the President's moral critics. They delighted in stealing our ammunition and shooting us with it. "Hypocrites," they cried, "what gives you the right to judge the man, the wife, and the mistress? Leave them alone. Mind your own business. Get the log out of your eye!"

Conversation prolonged due to lack of consensus.

What is the meaning of Jesus' words in Matthew 7:1? How do we apply this scripture to the world of our day? How do we treat the sins of our brethren, our neighbors, and our leaders?

The answer begins with how we treat the sins of self. Before we can evaluate the sins of the world, we must first recognize our own sinful condition. This is followed by a commitment to increased holiness. As we plead for mercy that God will not treat us as we deserve (Psalm 103:6-14), we become folks who are quick to dispense mercy to others. When we possess a realistic appraisal of our own unworthiness, then we have cultivated an attitude that is prepared to deal with others.

I believe that in this section of Scripture Jesus is addressing the hypercritical and self-righteous attitude of the Pharisees. Jesus is not instructing believers to suspend critical judgment, but to be careful not to become like the dreaded Pharisees who "trusted in themselves that they were righteous and viewed others with contempt" (Luke 18:9). What our Lord is warning us about is to stay clear of the harsh, self-righteous, quick-to-condemn style of the Pharisaical handbook. Jesus never suggests an indifference to sin and evil.

Jesus is not saying a reasonable portion of discernment and critical judgment is wrong. These are ingredients for good church sense. What is wrong is the ruthless spirit of the Pharisees. The kind of judgment we are encouraged to surrender is the merciless judgment of Jesus' opponents. In condemning others, they were in fact condemning themselves. Judgment is not the issue or the problem; the attitude of the Pharisees is the problem.

Scripture is a strong advocate of mature discernment. Jesus advises us: "Do not judge according to appearance, but judge with righteous judgment" (John 7:24). This is more the hallmark verse than Matthew 7:1.

The Apostle Paul mandates that we should "malign no one, be uncontentious, gentle, showing every consideration for all men" (Titus 3:2). But in the same chapter he clearly teaches that we must fuse our merciful hearts to sensible action. "Reject a factious man after a first and second warning, knowing that such a man is perverted and sinning, being self-condemned" (Titus 3:10-11). The rejection of a sinful character, as the one illustrated here, dictates an expression of judgment. Biblical judgment acknowledges sinful behavior that is self-condemning and labels it as such. In 1 Corinthians 5 and 6, the sexually immoral person is judged, disciplined, and expelled. The family is strongly encouraged by the church not to live happily ever after in their immoral condition. Everything is not okay, and to pretend so is to pervert God's justice. Judgment is mandatory, as is the proper attitude. "Brethren, even if a man is caught in any trespass, you who are spiritual, restore such a one in a spirit of gentleness; each one looking to yourself, lest you too be tempted" (Galatians. 6:1).

Work diligently to remove the beam from your own eye so that you will be prepared to assist others in dealing with their sin. And get that guy out of the spare bedroom and the intern out of the oval office.

Where Do They Get This Stuff?

With the exception of the County Road Maintenance Compound and "Uncle Charlie's Small Appliance Boneyard," the Smithsonian Institute proudly possesses the largest collection of used stuff in the known universe. Last year's bean counters inventoried 140 million items! It is a dust-bunny's paradise.

The Smithsonian's official mission statement is "the increase and diffusion of knowledge," but their warehouses resemble "the increase and diffusion of unwanted junk." While they strive to "collect, conserve, catalogue and electronically record" everything on this busy planet, their actual role in the grand scheme of things is to assemble a charm collection second to none. Their goal rings of nobility; the task is as mundane as cleaning up after a foiled weekend garage sale.

A number of questions come to mind regarding this mountain of discarded treasures and the folks who build display cases to show it off.

- ☛ How does one become qualified to serve as a custodian of abandoned cultural icons?
- ☛ Can you get a college degree in junk collecting?

- ☞ Do you have to intern at "Uncle Charlie's?"
- ☞ How many label makers do they go through in a year?
- ☞ Do the handlers wash their hands between species?
- ☞ Who donates this stuff?
- ☞ How does Goodwill Industries view its competition?
- ☞ Do they want my hair blower after my hair runs out?
- ☞ How did they choose between a yellow and a green AMC Pacer?
- ☞ Will the last curator turn off the lights and lock the doors?

Imagine the stress that accompanies the responsibility of insuring the happiness and comfort of 140,000,000 bits of stuff. Actually, it is not as burdensome as one might imagine, taking into account that ten percent of the collection is comprised of postage stamps. They are by reputation low-maintenance creatures. Lick them once a week and they seldom complain. Hubcaps and lava lights are also low hassle. In fact, most of the stuff survives nicely with a yearly polish and small dosage of Prozac. A 500,000-square-foot storage-and-conservation facility in Suitland, Maryland, built for $29 million in 1983, also plays an important role in keeping long-term tenants at ease. This year the 700,000-square-foot Dulles Center will open to the public, and history's garbage will have its prime forum. It promises to be the ultimate attic experience.

The single largest slice of the Smithsonian cache is its bug collection. These folks have gathered 30 million insects under one net! They must purchase chloroform by the barrel. It makes your son's third-grade science project seem kind of puny. We are talking about a quarter billion insect legs, unless of course, some of these creepy, crawling critters came from the remains of third-grade science projects, and then the count is likely to be less.

How can anyone ponder these numbers and not believe there is a God? Thirty million different bugs by accident, evolution, or unusually mild winters? I don't think so. They are a product of the curse that came with Adam and Eve's sin. And though they may be firmly entrenched at the bottom of the food chain, what they lack in social status they compensate for with raw variety. Be careful what you squish.

The long-term cultural merits of the Smithsonian's flea market fetish can be debated, but the fact remains that a lot of stuff clutters our world, and it is comforting to know that there are those who care enough to collect it. However, at some point in time, one has to wonder if a case can be made to throw some stuff away. It has to be difficult justifying the amount of precious space an AMC Pacer occupies. Ten million centipedes could frolic in that turf. Will our great-grandchildren profit from perpetuating the Pacer boondoggle? Do we really need to keep a Veg-O-Matic under glass? How many rodents are enough? Perhaps the Smithsonian ought to consider a good old-fashioned spring cleaning and get rid of some of that junk.

Perhaps the church should do the same thing once in a while.

The Smithsonian collects bugs and kitchen gadgets; we collect traditions and customs. Much of what we have assembled over the centuries is valuable, but some of the stuff ought to be thrown out; it has no value outside of collecting dust. As curators of Christ's precious body on earth, it makes good church sense that we function as responsible stewards. There is no place in the Kingdom for dead weight. The church doesn't need to carry useless artifacts from generation to generation and century to century. **Our great-grandchildren don't need a museum, they need a living faith.** Just because something works well for us in our space and time does not mean that we have to burden the next generation with dusting and polishing it. Veg-O-Matics were a cool slicing and dicing deal for a short time, but they have no place in the modern kitchen. Better stuff is available. Why drive a Pacer or a Gremlin when superior transportation is available? Get the beast out of the garage and use the space for something more productive.

The church doesn't have the luxury of maintaining a 700,000-square-foot warehouse or a legion of yard-sale fanatics and bean counters. We could better serve ourselves and our Lord by cleaning up our "act-tic" and streamlining our collection. Let's stick to the essentials!

Where Are You?

I heard a cute story recently about a grandmother who dug deep into an old trunk to find her childhood Bible. Showing it proudly to her grandson, she handed it to him for closer inspection. He examined it for a moment, and when he opened it a giant maple leaf fell to the floor.

"Look, Grandma," he said. "It's Adam's underwear!"

Not everything about the story of Adam and Eve is cute.

There are many adjectives to describe the tragic events surrounding the downfall of humanity's first couple, but cute is not one of them.

The Genesis account provides few details about the life and times of Adam and Eve. Instead it focuses on the primary event of their 930 years (that is a long time to live in organic underwear!). Adam and Eve are sinonymous with sin. They live in infamy for being the first to say yes to the devil.

The story of Adam and Eve is relevant because it is also my story and your story. Adam and Eve may have been the first to fall prey to the seductive wiles of the devil, but certainly they were not the last. Every person who has ever lived has been victimized by the evil one. At one point in time, we too, were synonymous with syn. We have all fallen, and if it were not for God's grace, none of us could get up. Sins 'R' Us.

Many intriguing details lurk in this ancient plot, and as always, hindsight is perfect 20/20. If they had it to do over again, they would play it smarter—or at least we think they would. Uncertainty looms as a possibility because of the uneasiness we feel in our own spirits. We don't have a very positive track record in regard to dismissing sin. We act more like eager participants.

Everyone of us seems to have a love/hate relationship with sin. We love it because it looks good, tastes good, and feels particularly good—especially when Satan presents it at its delectable best. We feel obligated to sample the wares. We consistently prove to be suckers for a slick presentation. A part of us wants to believe the lie, the false notion that God is not watching, and even if He is, He does not care. Bad thinking. God knows. God cares.

The other half of our schizophrenic nature hates sin and the Master Tempter who constantly exploits our vulnerabilities. We hate to do God wrong. We get disgusted at how easily we fall into the sin trap, time after time. It is like we did not learn a thing from our last beating. We appear clueless. We know the right thing to do, but we do the wrong thing. Brain dead.

There simply is no room for us to play the blame game with our grandparents who blew their chance to perpetuate Paradise. If we had been tending the garden, we would have done the same thing. It is our nature.

Genesis chapter three makes it clear that we all stand justly accused. We all have a sin problem. We are all as guilty as sin. None of us is righteous enough to hang out in The Garden. God cannot have sinners in his presence. His holiness will not permit it.

Fortunately, the story doesn't end with Adam and Eve's ejection from The Garden. God loves us too much to abandon us. We are given hope that God's grace will somehow prevail (because all things—even my reconciliation—are possible with God). The human story continues at God's will.

Listen carefully and you can still hear the voice of God. He addresses Adam with perhaps the greatest rhetorical question heaven has ever spoken: "Where are you?"

God knew perfectly well where Adam was—at the corner of 6th Street and Nowhere. He was up Rejection Alley, down the

Guilt Corridor, and around Condemnation Corner. He was lost. Bigtime lost.

"Where are you?" rings with grace. God makes contact. He is interested. The question implies He cares—cares enough to confront.

"Where are you?" means that the One posing the question knows where you are. He asks it not because he desires a compass point, but because he seeks a heart response. The question has purpose. It is the first step in a long journey back to Paradise.

"Where are you?"

God wants to know. Are you in a place where you can hear His generous offer of reconciliation? Are you at a time and place where you are ready to seek forgiveness and restoration? Where are you in regard to your attitude about sin? Are you stationed at a grace stop? Are you ready to accept God's provision for your salvation? Are you in a place where you can access God's redeeming love?

"Where are you?" At the foot of the cross, I hope. It is the safest spot in the cosmos.

What If They Work on Commission?

irens screech, lights flash, tires squeal, and motorists duck for cover. An ambulance is in the area.

I hate it when I get caught in the middle of an emergency. I simply want to get out of the way, but invariably I gravitate to the exact spot the ambulance wants to occupy. These drivers (every one a NASCAR wannabe) are professionally trained to make the rest of us look stupid. If I go left, he goes left. I go right, he goes right. If I jump the curb and hide on the sidewalk, I am high-centered in front of the house that called 911. I can't win.

I suspect that someday I will meet the Lord as a result of getting smashed by a frenzied emergency vehicle. They will run me over and call 911 to send another vehicle. They will give the wrong directions and I'll bleed to death on the sidewalk. What a terrible way to go out.

It happened again last week. I was cruising down Ten Mile Creek, minding my own business, sipping on the morning's second cup of coffee, grooving on some light gospel jazz, when the sirens, lights, and tires exploded into the comfort of my commute. I looked left. I looked right. I looked back. Nothing. I looked straight ahead and here it came. It ran the red light at I-67 and Duncanville Road, blinked right, turned left, and on two wheels rocketed up the entry ramp onto the freeway. About six other folks and I jumped out of our cars and sponged donuts, coffee, and mascara off our freshly dry-cleaned suits.

Another close call.

Shaken, but not stirred, I proceeded down Duncanville Road in an orderly fashion. I cautiously moved into the intersection at Danieldale Road to make a left-hand turn, when suddenly another ambulance was on top of me. Only it wasn't another ambulance. It was the same ambulance—running laps. They were lost. But they were lost at 70 mph! I saw the passenger paramedic pointing right as the driver jerked the wheel left. Even the siren sounded scared.

Missed me again. I may live to see fifty.

I waited at the intersection until the accident waiting to happen disappeared in my rearview mirror. I imagined to myself, "What if those guys are simply bored and they are out on the streets initiating contact?" I feared the worst. "What if they work on commission?"

I don't want to sound ungrateful. I appreciate the fact that we have governmental agencies that serve and protect. I'm simply a little nervous about 70-ton vehicles speeding around the city frightening harmless morning commuters at 70 mph. All the lights, sirens, and squeals keep us on blinking red alert. Perhaps there is a better way to reach hurting folks.

Of course there is a church-sense lesson here. Oftentimes our evangelistic efforts are patterned after assault vehicles. We rush out to save the hurting with sirens howling and lights flashing. We speed past dozens of common commuters terrorizing their morning drive time. We are a little unsure of the directions, hesitant to go left or right, so when we come to the fork in the road—we take it. We are real bright, real fast, real noisy, real important looking, but often we end up running laps and accomplishing little. It makes little church sense.

Perhaps we would be better served by ministering to commuters in a steady, responsible fashion. We don't have to scare folks into the kingdom. We may be better off presenting ourselves as a rest stop on the freeway of life or a service station providing repairs and tune-ups.

Keep one eye on the mirror.

Only One Bidder

What would you pay for a piece of history? Some folks are willing to pay a hefty price.

In a recent national auction, a baseball enthusiast paid $3,000,000 (plus tax, title, license, and insanity fees) for one baseball (not the entire team). The ball is obviously a special piece of history—Mark McGwire's 70th homerun of the record setting 1998 season.[1]

Philip Ozersky, a St. Louis baseball fan, was the fortunate fellow who shagged Mr. McGwire's final blast. He debated for a short time what to do with the trophy ball. Many folks—including Mr. McGwire and the Hall of Fame—had keen interest in acquiring the prize. Virtually guaranteed $1,000,000 by the auction house, he chose to put it on the open market and see what some crazed lunatic would pay for nine ounces of yarn and horsehide.

Most of us rational-type, church-going folks shake our heads in disgust at such irrational profiteering. "How can any souvenir

---

[1] In auction lingo, the highest bidder is called the winner. In what has to be one of the greatest semantic coups of all time, a person who loses his/her mind and pays five times the actual value of an item is labeled the winner. What does it take to be a loser? Go figure.

be worth more than a Caribbean Island?" It simply doesn't make sense. "Who in his right mind would pay that kind of money for a piece of used equipment?" The answer: people with that kind of money.

Auctions are one of the most fascinating vehicles of a free-market economy. On the open market, true value is established, and usually the true value of an item is determined precisely by what some crazed consumer will pay for it. Is Mark McGwire's 70th homerun ball worth $3,000,000? Yes. Should it be worth $3,000,000? Probably not. Are George Washington's false teeth worth $250,000? Not to me. Are JFK's old golf clubs worth $150,000? Not in my garage. Are the memoirs of an Alamo soldier worth $330,000? Tom Hicks thinks so, and now they are on display at the University of Texas.

True value can be kind of a tricky thing. It is not always established by objective criteria. Not everything can be appraised like a house or a car. Not everything is listed in a "Blue Book" or can be assessed at the County Assessor's office. Some stuff has relative value: art, antiques, memorabilia, jewelry, chocolate cake, human souls. The value of some things can only be determined by the subjective impulse of the highest bidder. Value can be personal.

How much is the church worth? Three million dollars? Ten? A hundred? A zillion?

The church is worth exactly what someone would pay for it.

Blessed be the God and Father of our Lord Jesus Christ, who according to His great mercy has caused us to be born again to a living hope through the resurrection of Jesus Christ from the dead, to obtain an inheritance which is imperishable and undefiled and will not fade away, reserved in heaven for you. . . . And if you address as Father the One who impartially judges according to each man's work, conduct yourselves in fear during the time of your stay upon earth, knowing that you were not redeemed with perishable things like silver or gold from your futile way of life inherited from your forefathers, but with the precious blood, as of a lamb unblemished and spotless, the blood of Christ. For He was foreknown before the foundation of the world, but has appeared in these last times for the sake of you who through Him are believers in God, who raised Him from the dead and gave Him glory, so that your faith and hope are in God (1 Peter 1:3-4,17-21).

The church is worth more than all the silver and gold in Babylon proper. There isn't enough money in the Milky Way to purchase the church. There isn't a guaranteed line of credit in the cosmos that could bring the church home from public auction.

There is only One bidder for the church, One buyer who could meet the asking price. God, and God alone, could pay the price. He purchased the church and our personal salvation with the precious blood of his only Son. We are "the church of God which He purchased with His own blood" (Acts 20:28).

The church is of ultimate value because it was bought with the ultimate sacrifice. You are of supreme value because the supreme price was paid for your salvation. Call it the ultimate example of church sense.

Are you worth it? Probably not. Does God believe we are worth it? Absolutely!

We Sure Is Smart

*here is the wise man? Where is the scribe? Where is the debater of this age? Has not God made foolish the wisdom of the world?* (1 Corinthians 1:20).

We sure is a smart country. We got more wise guys and savvy gals than Congress has perks. We got thousands of geeks with big heads and cell phones. We got brilliant minds on both coasts, academicians systematically brainwashed by their secular mentors. And lots of them got important jobs at the universities. Some have tenure; they are the really scary ones. They buy test tubes and floppy discs by the case. They is an impressive lot. Well qualified to cram their liberal ideas down your throat. Sometimes us old-fashioned Bible believers are simply overwhelmed with their postmodern proclamations of cosmic truth.[1]

I gots to tell you, though, I sometimes find it kind of aggravating when these real smart folks say stupid stuff and expect the rest of us to go along with their shenanigans. I wonder to myself: **If they is as smart as they claim to be, then why can't they**

---

[1] This essay is more concerned with good theology than good grammar.

make sense of the simple truths? Now I understand that their credentials give them a leg up on the rest of us poor, naive common folks who still pray at school, and their impressive, sophisticated, gold-trimmed worldview is the darling of media giants and learned politicians, but if you is real dumb in the elementary things, then how can you be so smart about other stuff? It just don't make no sense to me.

I'm not implying that our culturally elite is all stupid; it's just that they believe and teach so many things that just ain't so. Sometimes I thinks that they ain't real honest with the evidence. I even suspect that occasionally they predetermine the result before they does the research. Seems like a waste of test tubes. This will frighten you, but it also occurs to me that some of our best brains are so full of biases that they can't think straight. And some of the real movers and shakers of modern thought have some personal agendas. Others aren't what you would exactly call morally upright. Imagine that! I think we just got to be real careful dealing with folks who claim to be real smart, but work real hard to promote stuff that don't ring with truth. Makes me as nervous as a long-tailed cat in a room full of rocking chairs.

Take for instance, this century-and-a-half-old debate between evolution and creation. Old Mr. Darwin sure caused a ruckus with his fancy bird-watching down in those islands with the funny name. We've had nothing but controversy since. Darwin is dead and gone (and now knows for sure there is a God of creation), but he left us with a mess. And we ain't made a lot of progress.

It strikes me as downright amazing that so many smart people defend the theory of evilution. They preach it as the official, proper, and scientific explanation for the origins of the universe—you and me's origin included! Even the Supreme Court gets in on the action. They have essentially made evolution the official state religion. They don't want anybody to bring up this God thing. It might usurp their control. With a straight face they persuade us that we are nothing more than a cosmic accident, a freak of nature, a slimeball from the primordial gene pool. It's just a matter of odds and billions of centuries, they claim. Call it primitive luck. Crank of the blender.

Up in Kansas and Oklahoma they are debating the issue in

public again. The ACLU is up in arms. They got them some right smart lawyers, and they are gonna sue everybody—starting with God for meddling in the world. Smart folks are irritated that someone would challenge the status quo. "Violates church and state," they scream. "It just ain't right to talk about God." Ellen Goodman of the prestigious Boston Globe says progress has been set back a hundred years by the Bible thumpers. Makes me laugh, 'cuz some folks takes Ellen seriously.

It seems that the Kansas State Board of Education ain't so convinced that something came from nothing without Divine intervention. This type of rhetoric and thinking really puts a burr under the saddle of smart folks around the country. Even the Governor of Kansas rose to the challenge. He got plum angry at his constituents who won't accept the theory of evilution as the only explanation for life. Governor Graves said that the decision to de-emphasize evilution is "so out of sync with reality." Now cut him some slack. He is under a lot of pressure from his wise guy peers.

It must not be easy being a real smart pagan. Primarily, because to be smart by the world's standards you got to deny God—the Ultimate Reality. That's a load. The Bible says it is "the fool who says in his heart there is no God." The pagan responds by denying the Bible is true. They make fun of Bible-thumpers 'cuz they say we is superstitious.

I find this accusation rather ironic. It is, after all, the unbeliever who believes that something came from nothing. If the Big Bang theory isn't the poster child for superstupidstitious (my apologies to that Mary Poppins fellow), then I'm a monkey's uncle (which for a creationist is rather a far-fetched claim). Excuse me, Mr. Smarty-pants, but I thinks it takes a pretty vivid imagination to swallow the evolutionary tale. Sounds like the kettle calling the pot black.

Tell me again about the part where Big Bang got the stuff to blow up. Show me again the transitional fossils that document macro-evolution between the species. Surely there is a jawbone somewhere from which you can construct an entire population. Explain to me one more times where conscience came from. Be patient with me because I'm kind of slow. But run it by me again how the Second Law of Thermodynamics dictates that we live in a universe consuming energy and winding down. It just doesn't seem like a fertile place for evilution.

I got to admit that I appreciate the evolutionist's faith. They call it science, but really it's faith. It takes a lot of blind faith to put your stock in evilution as the great truth. Christians would never gamble with those odds. One old dumb statistician said that the chances of mankind developing into their present state through the forces of Darwinian evolution is about the same as a tornado blowing through the city dump and assembling a Boeing 747 on the other side. Big time faith. You really got to want to believe it.

I think I is more suspicious than superstitious. I is suspicious that many contemporary evilutionists cling to their theory with such tenacity because they don't want to deal with the Ultimate Reality or Truth. "In the beginning God . . ." (Genesis 1:1). God is reality. God is truth. God is authority. I suspect that many folks are uncomfortable with a God who is in charge. They will go to great lengths, even accepting wild and wacky theories as truth, to avoid being held accountable to God, the Great Authority. When you are committed to doing your own thing, it is easy to compromise. Convince someone they came from a monkey, and there is little problem in behaving like one. The sad part is that mankind has had to surrender its dignity to receive spiritual autonomy.

I got to tell you that I am kind of proud of that bunch in Kansas that has stood up and told the emperor, along with his wise guy friends, that he is as naked as a fresh born jayhawk. Good to see common sense have its day. Makes us common folks feel better about the universe—even though we continue to grieve over the university.

Good thing us scientific dummies got church. We just couldn't compete in the real world—too far out of sync. Seems to me that out of sync is the place to be. Doesn't look like the future is real bright for those marching to the pagan beat. I thank God for simple and Ultimate Reality. I'll stick with church sense.

Destroying a Good Thing

My wife loved her new kitchen floor. A trendy shade of harvest gold with splashes of orange and royal blue, it coordinated perfectly with the new stove and fridge wedged between freshly painted cabinets. Granted, the pattern stamped on the vinyl canvas was not fresh from the brush of Michelangelo, but it caught your eye, and proved almost hypnotic if the morning sun glanced off it just right and you stared at it long enough. Bright and cheery like my wife, the sparkling new floor generated great pride as the centerpiece of her newly remodeled kitchen.

She had saved long and hard for the vinyl of her dreams, and although she spent too much for it in my opinion, it was her turf, and I trod upon it respectfully. A covenant was forged before installation that I would no longer rebuild transmissions or butcher large animals in the new kitchen. Following customs of ancient Eastern cultures, she furthermore suggested it would be prudent if I removed my waffle stompers and golf spikes on the porch. I received the distinct impression from the girl of my dreams that it would be safer to sandpaper a bobcat's bottom in a phone booth than to mess with her new floor. She reassured me her love for me was greater than her love of linoleum, but our marriage was young, and I fretted some.

The new kitchen functioned as part of a larger remodeling project, and to celebrate the completion, or at least the near completion (it's never done) of the make-over, we vacuumed the carpet and hosted a giant house-warming party to impress our highly impressionable friends. Folks came from far and near to oogle and google over our good tastes, artistic refinement, and superior craftsmanship. In return for their flattery, we provided an endless supply of food and drink, a small price to pay for affirmation. We needed each other.

Every half an hour another tour group paraded through the house. People appreciated what we had done to the bathroom, unanimously agreeing that indoor plumbing was the wave of the future. The family room received high praise for the cedar trim and "avant-garden" windows. The critics loved the dining room (but for the life of me I can't remember what we did—maybe it was what we didn't do). The men idolized the macho wood stove in the basement and the women cooed over the custom vanity in Sandra's half of the bathroom. All the guests raved about the stained-glass accents in the living room and saluted our domestic genius. It's nice when people notice.

In the final analysis, Sandra's new kitchen stole the show. Everyone adored her little corner of the world, and I could sense a measure of envy in the hearts of several who secretly lusted over her fabulous floor covering. "Maybe," I thought to myself, "it was worth the extra money."

This party differed very little from any other party. The women broke off and huddled together and chatted and giggled about things important to women, while, in turn, the men gravitated toward one another for thoughtful discussion of important stuff like football, fishing, cars, and golf.

The children were loaded with sugar and exiled to the basement to form their own social order because neither of the other two groups wanted any part of the little nose miners. The chemistry of a party is usually such that urchins are forced to survive on their own. Parties provide parents license to discontinue responsible parenting to the next appointed time. Parties remain the one place where old-fashioned values take precedent—kids should be neither seen nor heard.

The only significant difference between this party and the one in your neighborhood was the peculiar positions that the two special interest groups occupied. For some inexplicable reason, the male contingent and not the feminine alliance assembled in the kitchen and busily stuffed their greedy faces with my food. It was all right because as they grazed, I rambled about my most recent exploits on the golf course. They ate. I talked. Everything followed the script.

Nearly everyone loves my golf stories. Popularity in this realm can be attributed to several key factors. First, my athletic skill level is such that bizarre things occur on a regular basis; I make the unordinary ordinary. Secondly, my interpretation of the events contains enough fact to make it plausible, but is colored with enough fiction to make it entertaining.

As is the case with any gathering of ex-jocks and overweight duffers, one belligerent skeptic usually surfaces who questions the storyteller's rendition of the actual events. And it's really unfair. In this case it was my story, and I should have been able to tell it any way I wanted. They sat at my table, ate my food, and custom dictated they accept my version of history.

This particular evening, the antagonist demanded some sort of proof to support my tale. The others sided with him. Their hearts had grown cold from years of mutual lying, and they took their frustrations out on me. "That's an impossible shot," they clamored as I graphically related the miracle wedge from the rough on eighteen. "You can't get to the green from there."

Overreacting to the dare from my playground friends, I exited the kitchen to the unremodeled garage and returned boldly with my trusty wedge, itching to validate my manhood. This initiated a series of events that nearly cost me my wife and my life.

With the iron in hand, I politely asked the pressing crowd to fan out around the perimeter of the kitchen to provide necessary space for demonstrating the once-in-a-life time approach shot. To make the story authentic, I needed a golf ball, but rather than run out to the garage again, I grabbed an aluminum can from the counter and dropped it at my feet. It would suffice for the purpose of illustration. With the gallery at full attention, I dramatically recounted the complex shot. With the aid of precision hand gestures, I detailed the flight of the ball through nature's intricate labyrinth. The white sphere must sneak under the massive limb of the first tree (the doorway into the dining room), then immediately over the top of a clump of adolescent evergreens (the new chandelier from the Sears catalogue glittering majestically from its kingly position), then clear an intimidating sand trap (the half-empty punch bowl on the dining table), and finally fall gently to earth on the small irregular green near the clubhouse (the antique love seat near the bay window).

Arguably an impossible shot, similar to Watson's miracle chip from the rough at the U.S. Open, my better judgment suggested that it could not be duplicated in front of such a hostile audience. I ignored the warning. Blame it on testosterone. In a desperate effort to gather my nerves, I paused momentarily and explained to my cynical peers the proper technique. I related how the face of the club must be opened to get the ball over the second group of trees. They gazed in horror knowing full well that an open-faced sand wedge in the hands of a clueless amateur is a lethal weapon. Their anxiety deterred me little. The time for a dignified exit had passed. To retain credibility and reinforce foolish pride, a double-dog dare started must be finished. I had to make the shot.

The spectators sought cover as I began my backswing. As my arms came through the swing and the critical process of shifting weight to my front leg began, I lost concentration, distracted by a man scattering for safety under the table. His mad scramble conjured up images of a Lebanese terrorist attack.

The cardinal rule of golf mandates that a player keep his head down. I knew that, but when people are diving around the room, it is easier said than done. The scattering bodies distracted my normally precise timing. The result proved predictable. I hit under the can with a perfectly open wedge and the biggest divot ever constructed came up out of the new harvest gold floor like a NASA rocket and jetted through the first doorway before slamming into the chandelier and free falling into the punch bowl. The pitiful can hopped about six inches in the air and fell directly into the open-pit mine now located in the middle of Sandra's sacred kitchen floor. Had Arnold Palmer been there he would have beaten me to death with a putter. There would have been no resistance.

Total silence occupied the kitchen. As the gallery returned to their feet and tried to process the events of the last few seconds, all eyes turned on me in disbelief. How could anyone be so stupid? Their eyes then left me and focused on the small cavern in the kitchen floor, and then back to me in more disbelief. Then they stared at the punch bowl in disbelief. And then back at me in total disbelief. They wanted to remember what I looked like alive. In a death-defying culture like ours, one is never ready to be called home, but it appeared I had just hastened the inevitable.

The bad news testified that I had single-handedly destroyed a good thing — not the floor, but my fledgling marriage. However, the good news presided in that my homemaker wife and her loyal band of children-free buddies were too busy gabbing to notice the actions of her home-wrecker husband and host.

While a somber group of men gathered by the sink to write the obituary, my best friend predictably came to the rescue. His computer-like mind promptly formed a plan, not necessarily a good plan, but better than anything I had up my sleeve. This guy used to draw up successful plays in the dirt of grade school football games so I trusted his judgment.

Like a quarterback changing pass patterns at the line of scrimmage, he started barking audibly. He directed one man to grab the ball retriever from the embarrassed golf bag and fetch the flooring remnant from the punch bowl. He scurried another out to the garage to find something sticky. He sent a half dozen covert agents into the living room hoping to keep the women folk busy while "operation damage control" matured. Awesome was his middle name, grace under pressure. False bravado persuaded the male mass to trust his leadership for deliverance. What are friends for anyway? It was fourth and forty-nine, but confidence reigned in the potential triumph of this ill-advised "Hail Mary" wedge shot.

Fortunately, a new product called "Super Glue" had recently been introduced, and I had purchased a half-dozen tubes to have around in case of an emergency. This episode qualified. Reacting more to the adrenaline rush of my survival instincts than to the need for level-headed wisdom, I hurriedly squeezed all six tubes of Super Glue into the wound. It didn't require that much. I then wiped the punch off the vinyl scab and slapped it back into its original location. It fit surprisingly well. All the fellows nodded their heads in approval. I might get out of this alive, they agreed.

As we relaxed a moment to catch our breath and get our bearings, the vinyl prosthesis began acting in a manner suggesting implant rejection. The edges curled and the spine bowed its back. The busy floor pattern attempted to disguise the rebellion, but it became obvious the patch job required additional surgery to prevent staph infection. Oh, what tangled webs we weave when we hasten to deceive.

"Get something heavy to put on it," one man suggested in panic. "Got any cement blocks?" another asked. "How about an anvil?" chided the skeptic. "How about this?" my best friend inquired, removing Sandra's portable sewing machine from the hall closet.

"Perfect," we all nodded approvingly. A perfect specimen, the fifty-pound sewing machine with the turquoise daisy pattern "contact paper" cabinet was strategically placed on the damaged area. We collectively drew a sigh of relief thinking we had pulled a fast one on Sandra and the Grim Reaper. Men at a party are so clever.

The instructions on the empty Super Glue tubes promised total adhesion in less than a minute. Modern technology to the rescue again!

The tension relieved, we reassumed our party mentality and were having a grand time when slowly I began to sense a strange and ominous presence in the room. It was Sandra.

Along with her entourage, they ventured into the kitchen to get a fair share of the food currently monopolized by the men. One of the gals with too much punch in her blood tripped over the misplaced sewing machine and fell flat on her face on Sandra's new floor.

"What's this thing doing in the middle of my floor?" Sandra demanded of the group.

Unsatisfied with the seventeen humped shoulders and thirty-four lying eyes that greeted her inquiry, she unremittingly searched out her husband in the sea of innocent faces. As we made eye contact, she gave me that look that said "if you embarrass me in public again I'll skin your hide." She smiled sweetly at the others. "This old beast belongs in the closet."

She reached for the handle and every man in the room bowed his head in silent prayer that the Super Glue would fulfill its part of the bargain.

Super Glue, like so many products, is only as effective as the one who administers it. You can't blame Super Glue for human error. It did its job. I failed mine.

When the fifty-pound sewing machine was placed on the repaired area, the excess glue from the five additional tubes quickly attached itself to the bottom of the cabinet. It bonded. The sewing machine and the floor were one.

Sandra casually stooped to pick-up the machine, but it refused to budge from its new home. She pulled harder. Still no response. She jerked once. She jerked twice. On jerk number three, the seventeen jerks involved in the foiled conspiracy dove for cover once again. She overpowered the bulky cabinet. Idaho farm girls are seldom intimidated by large inanimate objects, and the beast surrendered. By now, everything in the room but the sewing machine was extremely animate and running for the door. The full wrath of a good woman married to a dipstick man was about to be unleashed.

She eventually yanked so hard that when it broke loose she was hurled backward in the pathetic fashion of Charlie Brown when Lucy pulls the football away at the last moment. She landed horizontally on the new harvest gold floor next to her unconscious friend, pinned convincingly to the mat for a three count by a sewing machine. A most unfortunate climax to a most unfortunate turn of events, my sin was discovered.

Trying to bring a little levity to a potentially stressful situation, I asked my spousal-unit, "Now, Honey, why did you want to go and ruin your new floor like that?"

The floor divot was now twice its original size and stuck firmly to the bottom of the ugly old sewing machine cabinet. A team of oxen couldn't separate the two.

My wife didn't require a full explanation of the facts to conclude that I was somehow the chief perpetrator of the crime. Standing there with a sand wedge still glued to my right hand and a sorry look on my face, I mumbled something about the pain of a double bogey.

At this juncture, the story takes an unexpected turn. Rather than pummeling me about the head and shoulders with my own golf club, my wife instead began laughing uncontrollably. She threw her arms around my neck and hugged me. She caught her breath, gazed intently at the fish pond located in her new floor, and broke out laughing again. "It's okay, Honey," she said, "you can buy me a new kitchen tomorrow."

"Avocado green?" I asked.

Sandra and I have been married for twenty-five years, and we've prospered through good times and bad times, not because I'm a good person always doing good things, but because she is willing to forgive. We've stayed happily married because early on she made a decision out of the goodness of her heart to forgive me, and forgive me, and forgive me . . . seventy times seven!

I'm a klutz. I'm a dipstick. I'm a jerk at times. So is Sandra. So are you. So is your spouse. None of us are perfect. We all make mistakes. We all stumble and fall at times. We are all human, and sometimes being human ain't all that tidy. In fact, sometimes it's darn messy. And if there is one thing we all desperately need—it's forgiveness.

In an unforgiving world, the church's biggest draw may be its willingness to practice biblical forgiveness. Forgiveness surpasses common sense. It epitomizes vintage church sense. If we can remember that God forgave us when we were as guilty as sin, perhaps we will be quick to forgive others in like fashion. Such mercy will overwhelm even the biggest jerk.

Watch Where You Walk

I haven't seen a pair of free Cowboy tickets since they started winning Super Bowls. But it didn't used to be this way. Back in the late 1980s before Jerry, Jimmy, Emmitt, and Troy, when da' 'Boys stunk up the joint and went 1-15, free tickets were everywhere. It is no exaggeration to say that season ticket holders couldn't find enough friends to give away all the tickets. Texas Stadium was not the place to be.

A joke circulated around the city about a couple who went to the West End for dinner on a Saturday night, and when they returned to the parking lot, they found their car's windshield smashed. Someone had broken in and laid a pair of Cowboy tickets on the dash.

I used to go to a lot of Cowboy games in the late '80s. I wasn't smart enough to know that it wasn't the place to be. I thought I got guest tickets because friends and neighbors thought I was worthy. I was as clueless as the Cowboys.

Back then Texas Stadium was dry; no alcohol was sold on the premises. However, when the home team was 1-15 and everyone in attendance was there on a free ride, the ushers looked the other way as dejected fans eased their pain by self-medicating from a flask. Even though the local 'Boys were out of most games by the third quarter, three quarters of the fans were too drunk to care.

I specifically remember exiting a game in 1989 when everyone around my boys and me was so tipsy they were struggling to find the gate. In particular, there were a couple of dads, with a stable of boys, who were too drunk to walk—much less drive. They were bouncing off each other and the walls when suddenly a couple of their rambunctious sons darted in front of their path. Unable to apply the brakes in a timely fashion, they stumbled over the boys, tilted forward, short of a first down, and promptly fell on their helmetless faces, their chins simultaneously bouncing off the concrete.

It was the best tackle I had seen all day.

One of the men, shaken but conscious, rolled over, pulled himself to a sitting position, made eye contact with his son, the wannabe linebacker, and gathered the strength to launch into a long and profane tirade directed at the boy who had moments ago sent him sprawling down Aisle 221.

Wiping the blood from his face with a dirty napkin, he concluded his sentiments with this admonition: "For Christ's sake, boy, watch where you are walking!"

The hair on the back of my neck stood up. I looked around for a yellow flag. There is never a referee around when you need one. I considered finishing the job his boys had started, but I figured the Lord could handle a common blasphemer on his own. I huddled with my own brood. We executed a flanker reverse to perfection and sprinted for the car, only to find we had to compete with 40,000 drunks for a space on the Interstate.

Sitting in the car, reflecting on the events of the past few minutes, it dawned on me that the battered fullback, who had spilled his blood in Aisle 221, had accidentally spoken truth and made good church sense. Intending to curse the Lord, the Cowboys, the concrete, the boys, and the Special Prosecutor, he had actually quoted some important scripture. Talk about the Lord bringing good out of evil!

"For Christ's sake, boy, watch where you are walking!" (Ephesians 5:15).

We are admonished throughout Scripture to walk (that is, to live) in the light of Christ's reality and truth. We are obligated to make the most of the opportunities before us in this evil age

(Ephesians 5:16). The will of the Lord is for us to pattern our walk after His—loving, caring, helping, holding, teaching, supporting (5:2-17).

It is also noteworthy that this brief Scripture closes (v. 18) with a warning to be filled with the Spirit, not with the spirit of strong drink! Fans everywhere, take note!

The church is engaged in the ultimate walk-a-thon. We are walking in the steps of Jesus, wherever they lead. Free tickets to heaven are available for those who choose the path of righteousness.

This Polluted
Commuted Mess

Obviously, we have a problem. You can't get there from here—at least at 8 a.m. or 5 p.m. Commuters outnumber roads a million to one.

Over five million people reside in the Dallas-Ft. Worth Metroplex. Many of these dazed and confused motorists are obligated to duties on the north side while living on the south side. Same goes for east-side and west-side folks. They all meet somewhere in the middle and it is a mess.

It is like playing Chinese Checkers with eight people. There are more marbles than there are holes. There are no shortcuts. The whole maze is under construction. Freeways are more like slaveways. It ain't a pretty sight.

And it is going to get worse. Public officials tell us that the DFW area will grow by more than 100,000 people a year for the next twenty years. Oh, goody, goody. Pass the shoehorn.

A recent two-page map in the *Dallas Morning News* outlines current and projected road construction. Billions of dollars and zillions of delays. In a hurry? Forget it.

Welcome to the world of "Urban Sprawl."

Sociologists, demographic experts, and overrated suburban planners assure us that Urban Sprawl promises great hassles for the twenty-first century.

Cities are getting bigger and broader. Folks are moving farther out. Commutes are getting longer. Tempers are getting shorter. Gridlock waits for no man. Pollution is worse. The EPA threatens to cut off federal funds to big, hot, southern cities that don't clean up their acts and their air. Everyone thinks their neighbors ought to support and ride public transit. Sales of SUVs are at record levels.

Being part of the problem makes me feel important. Like you, I am Mr. Urban Sprawl. It is nice to be noticed.

Though I make no claims to being an expert in the emerging science of Urban Sprawl, I am a typical pundit with some ideas on how to manage this polluted commuted mess:

1) *All women are prohibited from applying makeup in traffic.* Any female commuter caught violating this law will be fined $10,000 and assigned 1,000 hours of community service collecting trash along the freeway. Plus, no mascara for one year.

2) *All men are prohibited from transporting old mufflers, old tires, old carpet, or old pallets in any pickup truck older than they.* Violators will be exiled to Minnesota. They will never notice. The world will be a better place.

3) *All teenage drivers must start in the slow lane and stay there for the duration of their journey.* Any young daredevil caught weaving in congested traffic over 70 m.p.h with music playing over 70 decibels will be assigned double algebra homework and issued a bicycle. Triple homework if they act stupid.

4) *Any person, man, woman, or adult wannabe, who pulls a trailer without working tail lights will be banned from Urban Sprawl for life.* Their vehicles will be seized and impounded and the trailer sliced into rebar for future freeway construction. No exceptions.

5) *Anyone caught driving without adequate liability insurance will be automatically at fault for everything.* They will be forced to work every Saturday in a rebar plant slicing up confiscated trailers until their bills are paid.

6) *Folks who continually operate a cell phone in a hazardous fashion will forfeit all driving privileges and become regular public transit customers where they will be assigned their own bus full of other talkers—kind of a cell phone hell.*

7) *Any motorist whose driving irregularities are a result of a poor night's sleep because the neighbor's dog barked all night is immune from accountability.*

8) *Everyone must go to church on Sunday.* Church has proven to reduce stress from the hassles of Urban Sprawl. Folks who attend church on a regular basis have a tendency to be gentler, kinder, and increasingly patient, even more tolerant of other Sprawlers. Church sense teaches fundamental coping skills, including the golden rule. People in church on Sunday are less likely to get hot under the collar on Monday. They prefer the role of peacemaker over warmonger. Long-time church folks grow more responsible, even to the point of looking out for the best interests of others. Church can solve a lot of problems.

Maybe we ought to build more churches and less freeways. Makes sense.

Then One Day

Let me tell y'all a story
'bout a man named Jed,
a poor mountaineer,
barely kept his family fed.
And then one day, he was
shootin' at some food,
when up through the ground
come a-bubblin' crude,
oil, that is, black gold, Texas tea.
Well, the first thing ya' know
ol' Jed's a millionaire,
his kinfolks said, 'Jed, move away from there!'
They said, Californee is the place ya' oughta' be,
So he loaded up his truck
and moved to Beverly,
Hills, that is, swimmin' pools, movie stars.

Theme song from *The Beverly Hillbillies*

I still watch it, late at night, grazing through the channels, when no one else is around. I know a stupid show when I see one, but it never promoted itself as anything else. Jethro, Granny, and Ellie Mae are my old friends. We grew up together, and if I hadn't married Sandra, I would likely still have a crush on Ellie Mae!

The Beverly Hillbillies format was a classic situational comedy, a bunch of country hicks relocated among the snooty snobs of upscale Beverly Hills. They didn't belong, but they didn't know it, and they didn't care! They reckoned the natives had the problem! They were there on a fluke, but they still had to be reckoned with, and folks like Mr. Drysdale had to learn to deal with them.

Have you ever considered how the Clampett clan was able to leave the hills and join the Hills? Jed was out shooting at critters one day, just like he had done for the fifty years before the big day, when a stray bullet hit the motherload. He was simply doing what he was supposed to be doing and what he had been doing for years, when all of a sudden—Bingo! He hit the big one. His tanker came in.

Isn't that the way it goes sometimes? Especially when you are busy about God's work.

Consider a number of the characters that make up the early chapters of the book of Luke. Common folks. Doing their jobs. Minding their own business. Sensitive to the blowings and goings of the Spirit. Taking it a day at a time, with a certain expectation that one day God would do something very special. But patient and steady. Many old and worn and about out of days, but full of hope. "But then one day he was shootin' at some food, and. . ." Then one day. Then one day:

Zacharias . . . A faithful priest carrying out his duty at the temple.

Elizabeth . . . A barren woman past her prime, haunted with the shame of an empty home, but still praying.

Mary . . . A sheltered young girl blossoming into womanhood, busy with chores on a country farm.

Joseph . . . A humble carpenter trying to scratch out a living and save a few pennies to start a family.

Shepherds . . . Working the late shift and struggling to stay
awake are suddenly accosted by an angel.

Simeon . . . An old graybeard, hanging around the temple
grounds for decades waiting for the consolation of
Israel, bumps into Jesus' family on their way to sacrifice a couple of young pigeons.

Anna. . .The prophetess has seen thousands of little boys
come and go from the temple in her eighty-four
years, but this boy is different. The redemption of
Israel has become flesh.

God works in mysterious ways. Before the foundations of the
worlds were laid, He purposed to send forth his son into the
world to redeem his special creation plagued by sin (Ephesians
1:3-14*)*. Thousands of years passed, the sun rising in the east and
setting in the west day after day, rain falling on the just and the
unjust, people born, people passing, life going on. Then one day,
at the right time, God sent forth his son into the world (Galatians
4:4-5).

The incarnation of God in the flesh caught most folks off
guard. The possibility may have circulated somewhere in the deep
recesses of their minds, but for almost everyone it was not a
front-and-center possibility. Understand that these early folks
were a lot like us. They had heard rumors that God was alive and
well and acting on their behalf, but they never considered that
today may be the day that He comes near. God is frequently the
God of history and the God of the future, yet infrequently our
God of the present. But then one day . . . .

Routine is both friend and foe. It brings us order, gives us
purpose, keeps us out of trouble for the most part, and turns our
days into years. Yet, it can manipulate us into habitual patterns
that close our eyes to possibilities. Routine can become so natural that we forget about the supernatural. It is eternally important
that as we go about the day-to-day business of life, we keep our
eyes and hearts open to God's constant activity.

Church has many important functions in the believer's life,
but few are of more value than her role in keeping disciples on
edge.

Jesus is coming again, and it might be today, so be ready. Therefore encourage one another, and build up one another with these words (1 Thessalonians 4:13-5:11, author's paraphrase).

For we are God's fellow workers; you are God's field, God's building. Do you not know that you are a temple of God, and that the Spirit of God dwells in you? (1 Corinthians 3:9,16).

Be on the alert, stand firm in the faith, act like men, be strong (1 Corinthians 16:13).

Remember, faithful is He who calls you, and He also will bring it to pass (1 Thessalonians 5:24).

Church sixth sense whispers to our hearts that we ought to be ready for something special.

Then one day, God is going to do His deal in your life. Will you be ready? Will you even notice? Will you care?

Soft and Sweet

W e all stumble in many ways. If anyone is never at fault in what he says, he is a perfect man, able to keep his whole body in check. When we put bits into the mouths of horses to make them obey us, we can turn the whole animal. Or take ships as an example. Although they are so large and are driven by strong winds, they are steered by a very small rudder wherever the pilot wants to go. Likewise the tongue is a small part of the body, but it makes great boasts. Consider what a great forest is set on fire by a small spark. The tongue also is a fire, a world of evil among the parts of the body. It corrupts the whole person, sets the whole course of this life on fire, and is itself set on fire by hell. All kinds of animals, birds, reptiles and creatures of the sea are being tamed and have been tamed by man, but no man can tame the tongue. It is a restless evil, full of deadly poison. With the tongue we praise our Lord and Father, and with it we curse men, who have been made in God's likeness. Out of the same mouth come praise and cursing. My brothers, this should not be. Can both fresh water and salt water flow from the same spring? My brothers, can a fig tree bear olives, or a grapevine bear figs? Neither can a salt spring produce fresh water (James 3:2-12).

Normal babies play with rattles. Others cuddle with stuffed animals. Many little tykes like plastic bikes, miniature Jordan Nikes, and the likes. But not our boy.

For his first birthday he demanded a "doo-da-doo" (screwdriver) and a "hammo" (hammer), and not some cheap, plastic, Fisher-Price imitation. He wanted a Tru-Value, long shaft, Phillips head, real deal screwdriver with a red and yellow handle. His hammo of preference was a left-handed, 14 oz. Stanley claw with a textured blue rubber grip. Tim Allen proved popular at our house long before America discovered "Tool Time."

For a one-year-old, wannabe carpenter, Mesa was remarkably adept at swinging a hammo. I built him a wooden peg stool, and he would hammer the square pegs through the round holes, turn it over, and beat them back the other way. He would do this for hours, or until the pegs cried uncle and begged for mercy. Friends and neighbors used to watch in amazement as the little southpaw pounded the helpless dowels into submission. He was so cute.

Cute seldom lasts forever. In our parental bliss, we forgot that the hammer also possessed (along with the infant!) a destructive quality.

One quiet Saturday afternoon while the boy's mother and I were resting (exhausted from chasing the little burner), he set about the business of destroying the house with his hammo. Beginning with the cheap plastic stuff that occupied his toy box, he moved on to bigger game like televisions and coffee tables. To complicate matters, he discovered the tool's expanded versatility and was thrilled with the effect that the claw-end had on glass and wood. By the time we corralled the disgruntled little curtain climber, our house looked like it had been in Sherman's path on his march to the sea! I vividly remember Sandra's glance in my direction; there was a suggestive nature about it, raising the possibility that the boy wasn't the only problem here.

Hammers are not evil in themselves. They have never been the problem. When used in the fashion for which they are designed, they are one of the world's great tools. Try building a house without one. Nails are unreceptive to blows administered by rocks or cast iron frying pans. Thumbnails take cover! Hammers, like many of their tool cousins, can be used to build or tear apart. They have dual ends and dual usages. How they are used depends upon how their masters choose to deploy their power. Mature builders use a hammer wisely. Immature infants use a hammer unwisely. Hammers are not the problem. Their swingers are the problem. Outlaw hammers and only outlaws will have hammers.

Tongues are a lot like hammers. They can build up, or they can tear down. They can be constructive or destructive. They can manufacture mansions, or they can smash thumbnails.

James, the bond-servant of Jesus Christ, consumes a lot of ink detailing the dual nature of the human tongue. With it, he says, we both bless and curse. He comes away from the discussion frustrated, stating that "these things ought not to be this way."

He is not the only inspired writer who notes the assets and liabilities of the oral hammer. In Psalm 52 David sings:

Why do you boast in evil, O mighty man? The lovingkindness of God endures all day long. Your tongue devises destruction, like a sharp razor, O worker of deceit. You love evil more than good, falsehood more than speaking what is right. You love all words that devour, O deceitful tongue.

The apostle Paul exhorts us as mature disciples to have Spirit-controlled tongues and speak words that are good for edification and encouragement. We have the power to build up or to tear down. We must learn to use our speech in a way that glorifies God and encourages others. May we be quick to construct and slow to destruct.

Remember the words of my wife's grandmother: "Keep your words soft and sweet for you will never know which ones you will eat!" Don't bring your forked tongue to church.

The Problem
with Dancing

But you, why do you judge your brother? Or again, why do you regard your brother with contempt? For we shall all stand before the judgment seat of God (Romans 14:10).

Periodically I receive an official questionnaire from a church or a brother (sisters seldom get involved in border skirmishes) designed to establish my orthodoxy in the faith once and for all delivered to the saints. I am not sure who or what invents these acid tests, but I sure get a kick out of completing and returning them to sender. Not only am I participating in important business, but the anticipation of waiting for word from The Council exhilarates the soul. I find it thrilling that there are those among us who care enough to interrogate.

The well-circulated, mimeographed form I received from a comatose church trapped in 1958 was one of the best I have seen in years. One hundred questions. All "yes" or "no." Explanations not required. Theology, cut and dried. "Just the facts," declared Councilman Joe Friday.

This particular questionnaire was special for a number of reasons, but most noteworthy was the fact that it did not mess around with peripheral issues like the virgin birth of Jesus, ful-filled prophecy, supernatural miracles, or the resurrection. Instead, it dealt directly with important things like microphone counts and left-handed clapping.

Some of my favorite questions on the exam tackled really big issues of contemporary Christianity like mixed swimming (I refuse to get in a pool with Labradors and Dalmatians), "Crossroads" (I always say that when you come to a fork in the road, take it!), and the precise definition of modest dress for women (I personally prefer Samaritan chic over Midianite swank).

It is hard to choose one question as superior over the other ninety-nine, but I think I have isolated the ultimate standard of faithfulness: "Is dancing sinful? Yes or No!"

Anybody who loves Jesus should be able to answer this in a heartbeat. It is as plain as the nose on your face. Obviously the correct answer is "Yes"; dancing at all times, in all places, in all situations, with all people is absolutely sinful, and anybody who thinks otherwise should be sold to the swank Midianites. After all, why did Nathan confront King David for his sin? Forget Bathsheba; it was because he danced before the Ark. Don't think for a minute that Jesus would be caught partying at a banquet, or a wedding feast, or a backyard dinner party where people kicked up their heels.

Dancing is dancing is dancing. No difference exists between a bunch of drunk, gyrating teenagers at a rock-'n'-roll concert grinding their pelvises against everyone and anyone in their zone and a faithful couple who celebrate fifty years of marriage with a little waltz in the privacy of their own living room. Folks in both scenarios are surely on a fast track to hell (and don't think God overlooks those weak moments when you danced vicariously with Lawrence Welk).

Clearly it is impossible to address the spiritual appropriateness of dancing with a "yes" or "no" answer. If Christianity were that cut and dried, then it would not be the scriptural Christianity we possess today. If dancing is always sinful, then so is driving (been on a major interstate lately?), golfing (more people killed and more windows broken every year on golf courses than dance courses), eating (try to convince a three-year-old that God made lima beans), and shaving (show me the necessary inference).

Dancing, like driving and golfing, is not inherently evil (well, perhaps disco comes close). God did not see fit to condemn dancing in the Ten Commandments. The problem with dancing, like eating and shaving, is not its innate moral status, but in how to apply biblical principles to the execution of an activity. Living a Christian life demands constant application of biblical principles for a person's individual circumstance. And this God-given individual freedom must be respected. "The faith which you have, have as your own conviction before God. Happy is he who does not condemn himself in what he approves" (Romans 14:22). I suggest that the dance police take the night off. Give it a rest, boys!

I can't believe a group of men in Tennessee or Timbuctu have the right or responsibility to legislate every aspect of your life or mine. With brothers like these, who needs enemies? **With brothers like these, who needs a Bible?** Just like I want to see the golden plates that Moroni supposedly provided for Joseph Smith, I want to see and touch the tablets that proclaim, "Thou shall not dance." Perhaps they also have in stock the original codex that established once and for all the divine length of skirts, shorts, and ringlets.

Executing the Christian lifestyle requires great focus, and it takes uncommon maturity and common church sense to do it well. Trying to legislate every little dimension of morality for others does not help. Folks have got to figure out most stuff on their own. Enforcing legalistic requirements on fellow Christians is not only criminal, but it actually retards Christian growth. Our time would be better spent in determining how Christ's resurrection impacts our lives.

The major problem with dancing remains with those wound too tight to pull the shades and give it a try. May I have the next questionnaire?

The Great Ministry

I n the recent process of reviewing a large stack of church bulletins, I came away impressed with a number of observations. I discovered that "Mr. Borrowed" is a popular author, that numbers are seldom *under*estimated, and that most preachers do not take as good a picture as do youth ministers (primarily because they have less hair). In addition to these obvious and common characteristics, the one interesting thing that caught my attention was the large number of different ministries and ministers that contemporary churches employ.

I found that there are ministries to the youth, the seniors, and those in midlife crisis. Ministries serve the down and out and the up and in. Ministers of music, drama, video, and home entertainment promote their agendas. Small groups have big ministries, big groups have small ministries, and average-size groups are often an embarrassment to the bulletin editor. There are ministers of assimilation and dissimulation. A growing list of ministers work with the disenfranchised, the disenchanted, the disconnected, and the discontented. Education ministers still play a role, but re-education ministers are in high demand. We have medical ministries, counseling ministries, chiropractic ministries, and diet ministries. And what about the preacher, you may ask? He is gone, replaced by a Minister of the Word.

I applaud our biblical emphasis on ministry, but I occasionally question our basic church sense. The majority of our developing ministries are good, but I am alarmed that we have ignored one of the most important ministries of all—the ministry of prayer. Not a single church bulletin I examined listed a ministry of prayer. What a shame. What a mistake.

The early church was short on official ministry, but long on prayer. The early church leaders recognized the central importance of prayer to a healthy body, and thus they designated ministers to care for people while they devoted themselves to prayer and the word (Acts 6:1-6). We would be wise to learn from their example.

I advocate that we continually return to the basics of successful Christianity, and that begins with a commitment to prayer. By instituting a powerful ministry of common prayer, much more will be accomplished for the Lord than if we employed a legion of ministerial professionals to accommodate our Sunday and sundry needs. Prayer appears to be the forgotten ministry; yet, if the church has any hopes of prospering in the future, we must first become prayer warriors on the battlefield of faith.

I am thrilled by the grassroots prayer movement in some congregations. I encourage everyone to become part of a small group committed to prayer. Those of you actively involved in prayer groups have a great opportunity to expand and bless others. Everyone is gifted for prayer. It is our single greatest untapped resource.

Prayer is a no-lose proposition. Folks committed to God and "devoted to prayer" are folks who change their worlds. Families that pray together stay together. Want to know God's will? Pray about it! Need better church sense? Pray about it. Make prayer a top priority and watch the blessings follow. Our church's success and your individual success are directly linked to prayer. Prayer is ministry, and it is for you!

The Fine Art of Grooming

novelist visiting in Dallas for a few days remarked, "There is only one operable verb here—grooming. It applies to the women, the lawns, the houses, the children, the dogs, the cars, everything."—Prudence Macintosh in *The Dallas Woman*

Proper grooming is a big deal. Billions of dollars are spent every year by fellow Americans attempting to look better, smell better, and flirt better. Television commercials are dominated by products that enhance our personal images and magazines are packed full of advertisements for grooming wares that promise miracles. We are now able to groom parts that I never realized needed grooming. I no longer glance through women's magazines because I'm embarrassed to discover what it takes to be a millennium woman. Grooming supplies on the shelves at my neighborhood drug store suggest I am missing important essentials to the good life. I sense I'm ill scrubbed. Do my peers think I'm a hick?

We are a culture consumed with making sure every hair is in place, every odor under control, and every nail filed, painted, and securely glued. *GQ* and *Cosmopolitan* are our handbooks to success. Martha Stewart and her cronies bully us into looking good!

What would we do on holidays and graduations if we couldn't give aftershave lotion and perfume? It is important to raise the next generation smelling right.

What's more, personal hygiene is only one dimension of the grooming issue. We also spend a lot of time and resources grooming our possessions. A visit to the Dallas yellow pages reveals that there are hundreds of car washes in the city. There are also hundreds of pet groomers and thousands of yard workers. There are dry cleaners on every corner, usually located next door to the hair salon. You can find experts who provide facelifts for buildings, landscapes, public projects, private concerns, and weathered grandmothers. If you want it groomed, somebody will groom it. Bring your VISA®.

Grooming is not an unusual concept. I only bring it up because of the excesses that almost always ruin a good thing. Common sense should find a better balance. We're grooming ourselves to death.

Have you considered the fact that average Americans spend more time blowing their hair than reading the Bible? Almost all folks are more diligent about shaving than praying. Fasting is popular—seldom to seek the Lord's favor—frequently to drop two sizes to look better in a new dress. People spend more time with a brush in their hand than they do with The Sword of the Spirit. Poodles get more attention than mission works. The average family spends more time working in their yard than they do in their church.

What we need is a priority shift.

Discipline yourself for the purpose of godliness; for bodily discipline [and grooming!] is only of little profit, but godliness is profitable for all things, since it holds promise for the present life and also for the life to come (1 Timothy 4:7,8).

We need to spend less time grooming our hair and flower beds and more time grooming our hearts. In the final analysis, what makes more sense? Does God judge us by our hair styles or the length of our nails? Is God impressed with a finely detailed pick-up truck? Are *Good Housekeeping* and *Allure* divinely inspired? Is your blow dryer really a gift from God?

We place a lot more emphasis on looking good than God does. We are a lot more concerned with cosmetic issues than God is. We are far more obsessed with the physical than God is. The Bible encourages us to store up treasures in heaven and not upon earth. Divine wisdom advocates that we tend well the issues of the heart, even to the neglect of our physical surroundings. Church sense pleads for spiritual attention where spiritual attention is due.

We are first and foremost spiritual beings. It is the devil that dupes us into thinking that the only things that count are how we present our physical possessions. Overemphasis on the passing stuff of this realm is simply sinful. And a waste of time.

Do not love the world, nor the things in the world. . . . For all that is in the world, the lust of the flesh, and the lust of the eyes and the boastful pride of life, is not from the Father, but is from the world (1 John 2:15-16).

Make time to groom your heart. Clean up your life. Weed out the sin. Polish up your ministry. Gird up your loins. Scrub your hands for service. Do the things you need to do to be a child of God headed for eternal life. "Set your mind on the things above, not on the things that are on earth" (Colossians 3:2).

They Think
They Are Right

e can't lay claim to the Great Wall of China, sacred renaissance art, or Hellenistic philosophy, but America has produced some pretty cool stuff on its own. Consider what we have contributed to the global culture: jazz, graffiti, rush hour traffic, drive-in burgers and fries, rock-'n'-roll, credit cards, baseball, three-day weekends, Archie Bunker, *Baywatch*, and Coca-Cola®.

Unfortunately, there has also been some bad stuff along the line: rush hour traffic, *Baywatch*, thirty-day-no-risk diets, disco, polyester leisure suits, the Corvair®, TV dinners, Woody Allen, *Dukes of Hazzard* pajamas, carpal tunnel syndrome, and liberal cultural elites.

And the last of the grouping may prove to be the worst.

Liberal cultural elites are not figments of our imaginations. They are real people in real high places with real weird ideas about what is right, just, good, profitable, sacred, and permanent. Though few in number, their influence is great. They have established themselves as the cultural and ideological power brokers of our era. Most importantly for those of us who advocate a Christian worldview, they are our chief competitors in the struggle for the minds and hearts of contemporary Americans.

Liberal elites often reside in the ivory towers of academia. For the last fifty years, many have scratched and clawed their ways to the top of our traditionally best institutions (then they get tenured, and we can't get rid of them). I believe a cultural crisis exists in many of our public and private universities. Many of the people in charge of shaping the minds and hearts of the younger generation are godless pagans steeped in Marxism and radical alternative socialism. Many are cynical, if not nihilistic, and their belief system is often characterized by a belief in nothing. By accident, and on purpose, they are about the business of eroding faith—faith in God, faith in the Constitution, faith in human possibilities.

These folks have a different agenda than us common folks. And they can be ruthless in the ways they exercise their rights and exploit their privileges. They are not opposed to rewriting history. In a few years they may revise history in a fashion that will conclude our forefathers and foremothers were not God-fearing pilgrims but godless pagans like themselves. They are intent on destroying the unique differences between the sexes. They are important promoters of hyper-radical feminism. Their views on the environment, personal freedoms, and individual rights are usually far left of the ordinary citizen. And, I guarantee you, they think they are right.

Many other liberal elites have found a bully pulpit in our political system. Our Congress, our executive branch, and our judicial system host an inequitable number of cultural leftists. They are relentlessly attacking the Constitution and seem to have a particular vendetta against religious freedoms and those of us who practice Christianity. From the ACLU to left-wing federal judges, we are confronted with folks who don't believe in traditional Christian morals or freedoms.

The entertainment industry boasts an exceptionally high ratio of cultural elites. Many of the folks who make movies, create television, produce music, fabricate superstars, and popularize culture are not traditional, Christian-thinking folks. Instead, many are bitter unbelievers intent on destroying godly values to advance their own self-centered causes. Homosexuality is a current example. The entertainment industry wants us to believe it is a normal lifestyle. They fill our heads with abnormal amounts of sexual confusion, violence, leftist causes, and general insanity.

Cultural elites from many disciplines and industries are united in their love for moralistic relativism. They like the idea of replacing God and objective truth with human reason and emotion. In a word, they love idolatry. **They see ultimate success as recreating God into their own image.** And they don't like folks who oppose mass destruction of the Christian system.

So what do we do?

First, recognize and learn about the problem. Become alert to the redefinition of culture. Work hard to reject the elites' definitions of tolerance, inclusivism, and pluralism. Continue to think critically.

Secondly, protect your children from the liberal crusade. Turn off the TV. Filter the movies they see and the books they read. Monitor their use of the Internet. Keep an eye on their friends. Be active in the school system. Check out their textbooks. Re-educate them every night. Send them to Christian colleges.

Thirdly, get more active in church. Spend more time in the Bible. Learn and promote the Christian system. Pray without ceasing. Increase your church sense quotient.

Fourthly, pressure your politicians into doing the right thing. Hold them accountable. Stay on top of what your federal judges are doing. Don't let them get away with constitutional fraud. Force people to tell the truth.

Finally, live righteously and seek first the Kingdom. Remember not everything you see on *Baywatch* is real.

Suckers for Gadgets

Following years of high-tech research and an investment of nearly $80 million, Gillette proudly introduced its finest shaving device to date—the Mach III™. Following weeks of nicking my chin, scraping my Adam's apple (a result of original sin?), and battling to reach the lip hair carefully tucked under my nose, I threw my new Mach III in the trash.

Gillette wasted their money, and I wasted mine.

New isn't always better.

New shoes hurt your feet. New styles seldom fit your body type. New teeth bother your tongue. New employees cost you money. New software has its quirks. New quarterbacks throw to the wrong spots. New recipes often bring you back to roast beef and mashed potatoes. New wine bursts old wineskins.

A new shaving sensation sounds great. Too bad it performs worse than "ol' reliable." I still appreciate my old twin bladed Sensor™ razor. The Mach III was like driving a Suburban™ in crowded residential traffic. It is big and clumsy and can't get through the tight spots. It may be designed to do 120 m.p.h. on the straightaways, but whose face has long, straight runs? Instead it is bumps and curbs and sharp corners and hairpin curves. Gillette engineered the Mach III for the Utah salt flats and my face is built more like Wolf Creek Pass.

But I'm always a sucker for some new gadget. I have a hall-way closet overflowing with remotes and sundry push-button devices. I have a garage full of mechanical gadgets that either broke the first time I used them or I wasn't smart enough to assemble in the first place. "Assemble yourself in only five min-utes with just a screwdriver and pliers" is the greatest lie ever per-petrated on the American consumer. (Just buy an unassembled backyard barbecue if you don't believe me.) I have a storage shed full of electronic wizardry that is planning a jailbreak the minute Y2K takes over the planet. (They haven't heard it was a false alarm.) Technological disobedience promises to be the curse of this century. **We have been duped into believing that new is always better, and that just ain't so.**

Now there is little argument that many new and innovative practices have benefited the way we do church. New song books, new audio systems, new Bible translations, new worship times, new evangelism programs, and dozens of other new procedures have made good church sense and enhanced our religious expe-rience. I am always open to the possibilities that new stuff offers. If something new will help us do something better, then let's do it! We can't be afraid of the new. But we can be selective and dis-cerning.

My grandfather never made the transition from farming with horses to farming with tractors. He refused to give up his beasts of burden for a beast that smoked, popped, and lurched. He was forced out of the industry. He got even by retiring. The world raced on without him as he and his peers gathered around the old wood stove at the Feed Store and reminisced about the good old days. He was threatened by change and the constant introduction of new stuff. I often understand how my grandfather felt. It is tough waking up in a new world everyday.

If you don't try the Mach III, you won't know if it is, in fact, the finest shave the world has seen. If I had not tried the Sensor, I would still be stuck with an old straight-edge monster that posed a daily threat. We have to give attention to new stuff in the bathroom and in the church.

The future is bright and loaded with possibilities for those who can navigate the channel. Our success as a body of Christians will be partly determined by how we filter new possibilities. With great wisdom we must decide what to keep, what to trash, and what to adapt. Good church sense will find a balance (see Acts 15).

New is not always better. Remember that God told Israel, through his prophet Jeremiah, to "return to the old paths." Not every innovation is biblical, practical, or expedient. In fact, a lot of new stuff is just junk and has no place in the Lord's church. Quick, get it to the trash bin! A mature church must distinguish between profitable change and unprofitable change. Just because Gillette or Pillette or Nillette invests 80 million dollars in a project does not mean that it gives our church a better shave. Sometimes we are better off to stick with what we have. Check it out, but if it doesn't work, scrap it.

Stop! Stop!
The Bridge Is Out!!

Friends don't let friends drive drunk.
National Anti-Alcohol Slogan

The greatest friendship one can have is to love one another
as Christ loved us.
1930s Bible Plaque

Have I therefore become your enemy by telling you the truth?
The Apostle Paul (Galatians 4:16)

Jesus said to him, "I am the way, and the truth, and the life; no
one comes to the Father, but through Me."
John 14:6

Go, therefore, and make disciples of all nations, baptizing them in
the name of the Father and the Son and the Holy Spirit, teaching
them to observe all that I commanded you; and lo, I am with you
always, even to the end of the age.
Jesus Christ (Matthew 28:19-20)

Religious intolerance is Un-American.
Hindu protester's sign outside
Houston's Second Baptist Church

Don't cram your religion down my throat.
My neighbor

Friends don't let friends go to hell.
Me

vangelical Christians find themselves in the midst of a serious dilemma. The mandate of Scripture is clear: born-again believers must share with others the wonderful story of God's grace. Specifically, that God has solved the sin dilemma by sending his son Jesus Christ into the world to die on a cross so that anyone who believes and obeys the gospel will be saved. Now if God could solve our present dilemma as he solved the ancient dilemma, we could get on with the business of fulfilling the Great Commission!

Just as the mandate of Scripture is clear, so is the mandate of many nonbelievers: "Leave us alone!"

Christians are caught in the middle. We want to do God's will. We want people to be saved and experience the joy of God's redemptive work. We want people to go to heaven. We want our neighbors to receive the blessing. But many of them don't want anything to do with us or our God or our church or our Bible or our love.

For sincere disciples who genuinely want what is best for their neighbors, this is a gut-wrenching predicament. How can we stand idly by while our fellow folks die and go to hell? Doesn't *agape* demand that we look out for the best interests of others? **How can it be in anybody's best interest to spend eternity in hell?**

Look at it this way. If you knew the bridge was out that crossed over the river outside of town, and you saw your neighbors load up their car and take off for the country via the bridge that no longer exists, wouldn't you try to stop them? Isn't it the neighborly thing to do? Even if they told you to shut up and stop trying to ruin their vacation, wouldn't you persist?

Look at it this way. If you were eating in a greasy restaurant and you saw a rat fall into the soup, wouldn't you alert the patrons to a bad stew day? Even if they were hungry and Wednesday's special was the soup of the day, wouldn't you tell them you smelled a rat?

We are creatures who are inherently wired with a warning mechanism. Just as beavers slap the water with their tails when danger approaches, so we instinctively watch out for one another's safety. Alerting people to the tragic nature of sin and the horror of hell is a natural response. It comes from our instinctive sixth church sense. We can't help it if we want to help.

The rub comes when our reluctant neighbors don't want help. What do we do when they accuse us of religious intolerance and gospel arrogance? How do we negate the idea that "there are many paths to God and spiritual enlightenment?" How do we treat our friends who are convinced everything is okay when we know perfectly well everything is not okay?

If we are serious about fulfilling Jesus' commands to convert the world, then we must find a way to bring people to the truth. We simply cannot allow ourselves to be paralyzed by others' resistance and indifference. Friends don't let friends go to hell!

I suggest the church consider these approaches to winning the world to Jesus:

1) *Live righteously.* Overwhelm your neighbors with honesty and integrity. Try letting them see a sermon instead of hearing one. Let justice and mercy roll down!

2) *Love your neighbors.* Love is the most powerful social force on the planet. Unleash it on your friends. Love them when they are unworthy and don't deserve it. Respect them as potential brethren. See them as Jesus does.

3) *Purvey hope.* In an uncertain world and an unstable culture, live confidently like you believe God's promises are true! Freak them out with your refusal to worry. Let them know that even though you don't know what tomorrow holds, you know Who holds tomorrow!

4) *Think evangelistically.* Soul winning is an attitude. Devote proper time and resources to saving the lost. Be a true friend. Really, nothing else matters.

Spinning Donuts

M ine was a '52 Chevy. Born a year before me, but treated worse. I paid $65 for the crippled beast; my overly critical peers thought I got ripped off. But it was my first set of wheels, and I loved it anyway.

The car weighed about 100 pounds more than the day it came off the assembly line, a result of body putty forced into countless fender crevices. Rogue field mice had consumed the stuffing in the backseat and most of the headliner. The bumpers were bumped out. Everything that contained oil leaked. I left a trail of grease spots from driveway to driveway. The speedometer had gotten vertigo and passed out the third time it rolled over. It generated only six volts, and not all of them found their way to the taillights. However, the car also had some problems.

The most aggravating mechanical flaw was the linkage that connected the steering column shifter to the distant transmission. It stuck. Frequently. If the r.p.m.s were not precisely correct and the movement handled with greatest of care, the stinking linkage would lock between first and second gear. This mandated an embarrassing and most inconvenient procedure, especially when trying to impress a date. I would have to pull off to the side of the road, kill the engine, muscle open the crinkled hood, and shake the living tar out of the devilish linkage. After wiping the grease off my hands, I would return to the pilot's seat, pretending that all cool cars, like cool women, required delicate adjustments. And then pray fervently the beast would start. And hope it wouldn't stick again.

The jalopy was dangerous. Local residents recognized this and gave me plenty of room to roam. It roamed because the steering was shot. The wheel had to be turned 270 degrees in either direction before any two gears in the oil-dripping gear box made contact and direction was reestablished. It was a thrill. Especially in view of the fact the brakes were bad and blinkers had not yet been invented.

In some ways, Sherman (nicknamed after the tank) was a type of SUV before they were popular. It excelled in the mud and the gravel. It was better off-road than on-road. All-terrain was its middle name. Dirt was its game. It went where new cars dared not play.

I loved to take the beast out on the dirt loading deck of the old mill and "spin donuts." A person and an automobile don't have to be very bright or stable to spin donuts, just reckless. Here is how it works (teenagers, close your eyes and ears and go to the other room): the driver enters the dirt area with maximum attainable speed and immediately after crossing the halfway line, jerks the steering wheel hard to the left. If the car doesn't roll over, the back end flies around and disengages solid contact with the planet. With the tires spinning wildly, the adrenaline-hyped driver pushes the pedal to the metal, holds the wheel tight, and the wild beast spins round and round throwing up dirt, gravel, and small creatures until a dust cloud the size of Rhode Island appears. Makes me excited just recounting it!

It is so cool.

For cars, but not churches.

Sometimes churches and church drivers are tempted to slither off the main road, find an old dirt pile, and start spinning donuts. When this happens, not only are good driving manners and sound judgment suspended, but so is simple church sense. They make a lot of dust. There is a lot of noise. Stuff is flying everywhere. It looks impressive, even cool in some folks' eyes, but in reality, nothing positive is happening. Spinning donuts has no redeeming value. It is a foolish activity for old beasts that can't compete on the open road with luxury cruisers. Going round and round in circles, even at high speeds, is pointless. It gets you nowhere—fast. All it does is create enough vertigo that you will likely pass out the third time you roll over. Plus, you can't be in the midst of a dust storm without getting dirty.

Instead, churches should resist the temptation of off-road shenanigans and stay on the straight and narrow highway to heaven.

Soot, Sin, and Suiters

Once again, I am convinced that fact is stranger than fiction when it comes to human behavior. As proof, consider the weird events that occurred at Lola Winder's house in Fort Worth awhile back.

According to news reports, Ms. Winder is a sweet grandmother who is a model citizen and a good neighbor. She is also raising a sixteen-year-old granddaughter whose vast skills include charming her male suitors.

One Tuesday evening Mrs. Winder tucked her granddaughter in bed, put the cat outside, turned out the lights, locked the doors, and went to bed. She was awakened from her slumber at 1:30 a.m. by the muffled cries of a male voice in despair: "Get me out of here!" (Then some cursing). "Call the police!" screamed the hidden voice.

She thought that sounded like a good idea, so she did. The police came, and together they searched for the voice's owner. They looked everywhere without success. Finally, an officer stuck his head in the fireplace, looked up, and saw two dangling legs. The intruder was stuck in the chimney. The Santa Clause wannabe had failed his first test.

Lt. Mark Krey crawled up on the roof and discovered love-struck Ben Jordan stuck in the chimney. It seems that he had come calling on Ms. Winder's granddaughter and sought entrance into the house through an alternative orifice. Lt. Krey reported that "unfortunately for him, the chimney was smaller than he was, and he became caught in more ways than one."

An hour passed, the whole neighborhood had been disturbed, and young Mr. Jordan couldn't be dislodged. "I was pulling my hair out," Ms. Winder said. "They were going to tear down my chimney and destroy my house to get him out."

Finally, Ft. Worth firefighters extricated him, and after the 90-minute ordeal, he came away with an injured leg and a bruised ego. He was charged with criminal trespassing and faces a year in jail and a $2,000 fine.

I'm not sure which was more undersized—the chimney opening or Ben's brain. Why would anyone enter such a tight spot when the chances of getting caught were so great? Call it flawed human thinking.

Why would anyone enter into an adulterous relationship?

Why would anyone take something that doesn't belong to them?

Why would anyone snort that first line of cocaine?

Why would anyone stay after work to juggle the books?

Why would anyone entertain the devil for dinner?

Why would anyone stay home from church!

We get caught in tight spots because we are sinful creatures, vulnerable to the schemes of the Evil One. Sometimes we remove our brains, set them on the shelf, and slither down the chimney. It doesn't make any sense.

Lord, have mercy!

And he does.

It is a wise policy to stay away from tight spots, but if you ever get caught, scream your lungs out to the Lord. He will pull you out of your trap, dust off the soot, and put you back on solid ground.

God is so good!

So It Goes

Identify the need; fill the need; make a lot of money. So it goes in American business.

Success stories surround us. Companies down the street and around the block are often started with marginal capital and maximum hope—and then sustained by a wing and a prayer. Capitalism at its best is a hothouse for possibilities.

I visited recently with a Christian businessman who shared firsthand his account of entrepreneurial capitalism in action.

He was called in as a consultant to help a new company organize its accounting procedures. The two owners knew that money was going out and coming in, but they had no idea how much, where, when, or why. They were shocked to learn they had made ten million dollars last year!

And they did it without a sales force. It seems their product, a relatively simple accounting template creatively designed to assist hospitals in processing new patients, sells itself.

"They get more inquiries than they can handle," he told me. "Customers are standing in line with purchase orders in hand."

He continued touting the distinctive quality of their product by explaining its popularity. "It sells itself," he said. "One hospital buys it and they like it, and they soon spread the good news to their friends who work at another hospital. They soon buy it, too, then they tell someone else. Understand that people love this program. They talk about it with evangelical passion!"

"Unfortunate," I thought to myself, "that evangelical passion is reserved for computer programs."

Some of the most energetic and enthusiastic people I know are businessmen and businesswomen. They are excited about life: turned on by their product, their idea, their company, their niche, their deal, their commission.

I used to work with a fellow who would get so emotionally choked up over a big deal he would cry. I have a neighbor who has been ticketed for cartwheeling down the service road after closing a land deal. I run from a local woman who is so hyped-up over her home business that she wears me out talking about it. She thinks she is saving the world. I got Caller I.D. a few years ago to protect us from a crazed in-law who thought her brand of diet supplement would cure baldness and dissolve kidney stones. She felt obligated to stock our shelves.

How is it that folks down the street and around the block are more passionate for the stuff of this world than we evangelicals are for stuff that transcends this world?

We evangelicals can learn something from the evangelical passion of our nonevangelical neighbors.

Folks talk about stuff that is important to them. They share the good news about products and ideas that make their lives easier, better, and richer. Their testimonies are seldom rehearsed; instead they are frequently natural and spontaneous. They believe, therefore they speak. They cannot *not* speak.

The mechanics of witnessing are similar even though the goods are different. Sharing good news corresponds to experiencing something good.

Perhaps evangelicals need a fresh shot of the Good News. Perhaps you need a fresh shot of the Good News.

The most obvious reason for not passionately sharing the Good News is that it ain't good with you. Have you somehow distanced yourself from the gospel? Have you let the fire burn out? Have you lost touch with your first love?

The single best way to convert a neighborhood, a community, or a nation is for individuals to get turned on by salvation—

theirs and others'. Return again to your birthplace and rehearse your transformation from darkness to light. Get that born-again feeling! *Emotionalize* the forgiveness of your sins. Remember the terrible cost that was paid for your redemption. Visit the first chapter of Peter, the fifth chapter of Romans, the second chapter of Ephesians, the fifty-third chapter of Isaiah. Understand and appreciate the genius and love of God in saving your soul! Personalize the Good News. Make it your story, your witness, your passion. Believe it! Receive it! Share it! "Tell the world what wonderful things God has done for your soul" (Psalm 66:16).

Christianity will sell itself if folks are given an opportunity to try it. As a purveyor of the Good News, you must speak from a heart overflowing with grace. "Let your speech always be with grace, seasoned, as it were, with salt, so that you may know how you should respond to each person" (Colossians 4:6). Make salvation in Jesus the most important issue of your life, and I guarantee that you will talk about Him! Identify the need; fill the need; make a lot of converts. So it goes with Christianity.

Stop It!

D*evote yourselves to prayer, being watchful and thankful. And pray for us, too, that God may open a door for our message, so that we may proclaim the mystery of Christ, for which I am in chains. Pray that I may proclaim it clearly, as I should. Be wise in the way you act toward outsiders; make the most of every opportunity. Let your conversation be always full of grace, seasoned with salt, so that you may know how to answer everyone* (Colossians 4:2-6, NIV).

Stop going to the grocery store to get groceries!

Stop going to the hairdressers to get your hair dressed!

Stop going to the doctor's office because you are sick!

Stop going to the health club to sweat!

Stop going to the service station to get service (as if that was available!) and gas!

Instead . . .

Go to the grocery store and tell someone about the Bread of Life and pick up some milk and cookies while you are there.

Go to the beauty shop to find someone who doesn't think life is so beautiful and share with them the truth that you can have a bad hair day and Jesus still loves you. Go ahead and get a trim as long as you are there.

Go to the doctor's office to find someone who is sick and tired of getting beat up by a sinsick world and tell them about the Great Physician. Go ahead and get your blood pressure checked since your yearly deductible is already met.

Go to the health club and seek out someone who is spiritually flabby and serve as their personal trainer. Teach them how spiritual discipline is profitable for all things. Pump a little iron since you are already in the gym.

Go to the service station and seek out someone to serve. Tell them what a gas it is to be a child of God. Tell them how they can get their tank filled at church. Wash someone's windows so they can see their way more clearly. And as long as you have your husband's credit card, you might as well fill your own tank!

The problem with our personal evangelism is the fact that we do not give it top priority. We have to learn to *think* evangelism first. Evangelism is an attitude, and we become adept at it when we make it job number one.

I am convinced that everywhere we go there are people seeking to hear a good word about God. The problem is me. I am not sensitive to the possibilities because I have not conditioned and trained my mind to look around and see the fields that are always white unto harvest.

Many times a day we bump into spiritually starving people, but we usually just bump off them, curse their clumsiness, and head to the produce section. We constantly stumble over people who are stooped and broken, but unfortunately we usually pick ourselves up, dust ourselves off, and go on as if nothing happened. We are oblivious to opportunity because we are more focused on specific tasks than we are evangelism. The church is void of new converts because we ignore outsiders. Church sense instructs us to cultivate a sixth sense for embracing the lost.

I believe that the Bible encourages us to evangelize as we go. Evangelism is not something we should compartmentalize and perform for an hour on Thursday evening. Instead, it should become part of our personality, part of our journey, part of our deal. Natural evangelism is most effective.

Jesus is the perfect model for natural evangelism. He saw people not in their clumsiness or sin, but for what they could become if grace could find a home in their heart. He viewed events and crowds as grand moments to introduce spiritual realities. He considered folks on the wrong side of the tracks as folks who might want to hear about mansions and crowns. He saw enemies and adversaries as wannabe disciples who only needed a little love and a little mercy. Jesus never went to a dinner party to satisfy his own belly, but to accumulate a group of hungry folks who knew they couldn't live on bread alone. He evangelized as he went.

Start today to revolutionize your world. Think evangelism first!

She's No Lassie

Summoned to the scene of a minor accident, I found the elderly couple leaning against their Cadillac shaking their heads in disbelief. Fender-benders are a way of life for Metroplex commuters, but the events that caused this seasoned driver to lose control, hop the curb, and bounce off an innocent live oak were most unusual.

"I've never seen anything like it," the white-haired man exclaimed.

"Nor have I," echoed his wife.

"I've lived in Dallas for seventy-five years, and this is the first time I have seen a fat black pig on a leash strolling down the sidewalk."

"It's my fault," his wife said. "I saw the pig. I screamed. I scared my husband and he crashed the car. I should not have screamed," she lamented. "He hates it when I scream in the car."

"It's not your fault," he countered. "I should be used to your screaming by now."

"No, it's my fault," she repeated. "I've got to stop screaming. We are going to end up dead in a fiery crash someday if I don't stop screaming."

"It's the pig's fault!" he screamed at her and the small crowd that had gathered. "What is a pig doing on the sidewalk anyway?"

He was having trouble disguising his anger. "Do they have a license for that pig? And what kind of a pig is it, anyway? And why are they dragging it around on a leash? Who ever heard of such a thing?"

He suddenly stopped the tirade, turned around, and started rubbing the big scratch on the front fender with the bottom of his suit coat. "Stupid pig," he mumbled. "Let's get out of here, Mildred, before we get attacked."

It was 1986 and Vietnamese potbellied pigs were the rage of avant-garde pet owners. The short-legged, wide-bellied, friendly Asian creatures sold for about $300, and according to many folks, made wonderful house pets. Supposedly they were easy to potty train, intelligent, clean, affectionate, and loyal. Owners appreciated their low maintenance nature; a once-a-day waddle around the block was sufficient exercise. As opposed to being dragged along by a hyped-out bird dog, cruising with a pot-bellied pig was a leisurely activity. No chasing cars or squirrels, no getting tangled in the leash, no stopping at every fire hydrant, and no sidewalk burns. It was, however, these public displays of pig lappin' that caused more than one auto accident.

I figured the fat fad had run its course and most of the porkers had migrated to the country or found boarding space in a back porch freezer. I had not heard much about potbellied pigs for the last ten or twelve years. I assumed they had fallen out of favor. That is why I was surprised to see a photo of a big pig staring up at me from the morning newspaper. The title of the article also caught my eye: "This little piggy went for help."

Here are the facts (which are stranger than fiction) of the story. JoAnn Altsman of Pittsburgh, Pennsylvania was stricken with a heart attack in the bedroom of her vacation trailer on Presque Isle in Erie, Pennsylvania. She couldn't move. Sensing danger, her pet Vietnamese potbellied pig, Lulu, wedged through the doggy door, somehow opened the yard gate, rambled onto the roadway, and plopped down in the middle of the street, refusing to yield to oncoming cars (I am not making this up).

By "hogging the road" so effectively that cars could not pass, Boss Hog finally persuaded a disbelieving motorist to get out of his car in an effort to get the pig to vacate the asphalt. Lulu would not budge. Frustrated, he hollered at the trailer, "Lady, your pig is in distress." Mrs. Altsman hollered back, "I'm in distress, too. Please call an ambulance." He did so and the drama had a happy ending.

As a reward for Lulu's heroic efforts, Mr. Altsman bought her a case of jelly doughnuts. It seems that pastries are a staple of her diet and one of the reasons she has ballooned from a four-pound piglet to a 150-pound porker in a year. The Altsmans had planned to give Lulu to their daughter, but now they think they will keep her around in case of an emergency. Good guard pigs are hard to find.

Heroes come in all sorts of packages. Not every hero is sleek and fast like Rin-Tin-Tin or Lassie. They don't always wear white hats and ride thoroughbreds. Sometimes heroes emerge in the most unlikely of characters.

Nowhere is this phenomenon more clearly illustrated than in the history of the church. **It is seldom the purebreds, the sprinters, or the Pharisees that possess heroic tendencies.** It is usually the country boy, or the wash woman, or the bespectacled mail room clerk, or the thief on the cross, or the tax collector who turns out to be the hero of the story. Church sense defies logic.

Just as there is a light side to the tale of Lulu, there is also a classic comic side to life in the church. Those who often look the part, aren't, and those who are least expected to exercise greatness often explode on the scene with a cape and an attitude. Church heroes can be the strangest characters. It is as if God delights in turning the tables, exalting the poor, weak, and bumbling, and constantly surprising us with a steady flow of Lulus. Be on guard. You never know what God is going to do next.

R.I.P.

thousand years before God called Abraham to leave his Chaldean home and immigrate to Palestine, a certain Mr. Otzi ventured from the safety of an Italian meadow to the high country of the Alps. There he promptly froze to death.

His Alpine grave lay undisturbed for 5,300 years. In 1991 two German hikers, following a popular trail through a 10,400 foot pass, spotted the frozen remains of Otzi (named after the Otztal region on the Italian-Austrian border) in a melting glacier. Initially thinking him to be an adventurous music teacher who disappeared in 1938, the world was shocked to learn that Iceman was in fact a flesh-and-blood link to the Copper Age.

To say the least, his discovery was astounding. Since he was in remarkably pristine condition, scientists have been able to reconstruct the life and times of Otzi.

He stood 5'4" tall and weighed in at 110 pounds. There wasn't a lick of fat on him, perhaps because he suffered from arthritis and chronic diarrhea. Hip before it was fashionable, he had fifty-seven tattoos scattered across his body, most likely remnants of efforts to treat a bone deterioration disease. His condition could also have had something to do with his diet. His last meal consisted of mountain goat, hard wheat crackers, and plums, no doubt the daily special at the Alpine Cafe. Otzi died at the ripe old age of about forty-five, alone on the mountain.

Like any seasoned hiker, the Iceman traveled well-equipped. He was dressed in leather underwear, tall lace-up moccasins stuffed with grass for insulation, a tailor-made goatskin shirt accenting fur-lined britches that drew tight at the waist, and a heavy grass cloak. He kept his head warm with a bearskin cap, suggesting to some archaeologists that he was more than a shepherd, perhaps a regal figure or religious priest.

His backpack was stuffed with important stuff: antibiotic mushrooms, a primitive lighter manufactured from a tube of birch bark containing embers wrapped in maple leaves, and a sharp Swiss Army pocket knife (without the red panels). He carried an impressive six-foot bow with a quiver of straight arrows. In the opinion of modern archaeologists, his most remarkable possession was his copper ax. This finely crafted tool separated him from prior generations of Europeans who dwelled in caves and beat their prey to death with sticks and stones.

Scientists brought Otzi down from the mountain and built him a new home in Bolzano, Italy. The expansive South Tyral Museum of Archaeology is an expensive $10 million structure dedicated to the diminutive Iceman. There he rests in peace.

Yet something is wrong. Even though scientists have done a superb job in restoring this slice of history, something is missing. An inventory list maintains it is all there, but the human observer knows better.

Clothing, weapons, tools, first-aid kits, and tattoos tell us something about the man, but without the spirit of the man, the picture is incomplete. "The body without the spirit is dead" (James 2:26). In spite of archaeologists' best efforts to make history come alive, it is a futile project because mankind—of any generation—is more than flesh and blood and tattoos.

Perhaps Iceman's greatest contribution to our modern world is to remind us that even the earliest prototype was fashioned by the creative genius of God. The God we worship and serve today created the world, the first man, and every human to follow. He breathes into every person the spirit of life (Genesis 2:7). The body is fashioned from the earth (to which Otzi clearly testifies), but the spirit is God-breathed. Remove man's soul and he quickly returns to the earth from whence he came. Otzi was God's man. You are God's man. You are God's woman. You are more than dirt.

I failed to mention one other item, a trinket found clutched to the Iceman's breast. Otzi died on the mountain clenching a marble disk tied to a tassel. It was unique among his possessions because it had no practical value. It couldn't slice or dice, dig or scrape, sew or sow. Yet in his dying moments, it was the pebble to which he clung.

Historical researchers call the polished rock an amulet, an ancient religious token, something more than a good luck charm, something less than the Bible.

I doubt that we will ever learn more about Otzi's spiritual orientation, but the simple fact that he had a spiritual orientation should tell us something. Otzi knew there was more to life than chronic diarrhea. The "God chip" implanted deep in his soul narrated not only his journey through the pass, but his journey through life. When the storm descended and life evaporated from his frail body, he looked up. Granted his faith is mysterious and imprecise (so is the faith of Melchizedek, Job, and Laban among others), but there remains an eerie link to our own.

Maybe Otzi wasn't on a secular mission when he got caught in the violent mountain storm. Maybe he wasn't out walking the sheep or simply scrounging for roots and berries. Maybe he wasn't simply on his way to an Austrian trading post with hopes of bartering his ax for a bag of magic beans. Maybe he was on his way to church.

Otzi was a religious man. What else but faith would take him on such a perilous journey through the high country? Would he risk life, limb, and leather underwear for any food other than soul food?

My best church sense guess is that he was on his way to a revival on the other side of the pass. He was certainly dressed in his Sunday best.

Archaeology is a fascinating science, but it always comes up short. It can't tell us much about the soul. And in the final analysis, what else matters?

Reveling in the Trash

Don't forget your purification from your former sins. Be diligent to make certain about his calling and choosing you. For as long as you practice these things (faith, moral excellence, knowledge, self-control, perseverance, godliness, brotherly kindness, and love) you will never stumble (2 Peter 1:5-11).

The official documents of the American Kennel Club have him registered as "Ranger," but at our house he is usually addressed as "No! Ranger."

"No! Ranger" is a rough and tumble giant Poodle with an attitude. He is getting saner and tamer with age, yet he is still on probation as a result of past criminal behavior. We are slow to turn our backs on him. Where Ranger goes, nothing grows.

Dogs, like people, have bad weeks, too. In a last ditch effort to mellow out the canine monster, I took him to the veterinarian and had him neutered. To get him in the car, I was forced to lie. I told him I was taking him to get tutored. He fell for it. Stupid mutt!

Anyway, I brought him home the same day, and after recuperating over the weekend (we haven't experienced such peace since the day he arrived), he woke up early Monday morning with revenge in his eyes and wickedness in his heart. I had tricked him with the tutor deal, but he was going to get the last trick and the last laugh. Stupid master!

After several days of suspiciously fine behavior, he struck on a Wednesday night. He lulled us into a sense of false security by pretending to curl up and fall asleep in the corner. Then when we were fast asleep, he snuck out of the bedroom and headed for the back porch and his favorite target—the garbage.

Somewhere past midnight we were awakened by a loud bang in yonder section of the house. Burglars would never be this noisy, so I knew it must be "No! Ranger."

He had knocked over our big steel garbage can (purchased to thwart his scavenging impulses) and savagely ripped open his prize. When I flipped on the light, I found the guilty beast with his head stuck in a Rice Krispies Treats' box, his stubby tail wagging in delight at his exploits.

In response, I planted my right foot on the littered tile in a fashion that would facilitate the placing of my rapidly moving left foot onto "No! Ranger's" exposed backside, but halfway through the maneuver, I discovered that between my right foot and the tile was a banana peel and an eggshell.

Dog – 2, Ron – 0. I recognized I was overmatched and limped back to bed.

It has finally dawned on me that our aristocratic, pedigreed French poodle is really a garbage hound at heart. His periodic fits of civility are a thin veneer masking his predatory passions. What is it about dogs that motivate them to sneak out to the trash at 2 a.m. and rummage through the stinking garbage? The problem with dogs is that no matter how much you groom them, train them, or lecture them, they are still animals governed by natural instincts. They are born to scrounge, and if you let them off the leash they will invariably end up in the alley reveling in the trash. Amazing that dogs are man's best friend. Or maybe not. The truth be known, we are a lot alike.

What is it about born-again believers that incites us to spasmodically return to the garbage dumps of our former life? **Are we, too, nothing more than debased animals governed by primitive urges?** Are we old dogs that can't learn new tricks? Is our Christian shell nothing more than a thin veneer masking our ungodly passions? Are we too undisciplined to be taken off the leash? Amazing that men and women are God's best friend.

Recognizing the vulnerable tendencies of disciples, many inspired biblical writers addressed this bizarre phenomenon. Time and time again, we are admonished by Scripture to insulate ourselves from our old selves that were motivated by base appetites of the flesh. We are repeatedly reminded that the old us was drowned in the watery grave of baptism, and we are new creatures with new minds, new passions, new standards, new identities, new commitments, and new lifestyles. We are no longer garbage hounds.

You should no longer behave like the pagans. Their empty-headed thinking ignores God, and they pursue a sensual lifestyle that is ugly and greedy, but in the end goes nowhere. Since you have learned the truth about Jesus Christ, you have a new way of thinking that produces a new lifestyle. You did away with that old rotten and self-deceived you, and now have been recrafted in the likeness of God so that you pursue holy living (Ephesians 4:17-24, author's paraphrase).

Christian maturity is characterized by consistent Christ-like behavior. As we grow in the grace and knowledge of Jesus Christ, we escape the corruption that identified our past life (2 Peter 1:4). Church sense promotes purity and nobility.

We are more than the sum of our impulses, more than animals. We are the prize of God's creation! Stained by sin, but redeemed and made whole by Christ, we have an eternal spirit created in the image of God. Jesus Christ rescued us from the garbage heap. He shook us off, cleaned us up, and transferred us to the palace. We have gone from the doghouse to the penthouse, from the pound to the temple.

There are few things as important to the future of Christian restoration as holy living. Unity is founded upon the gracious works of a Holy God and our commitment to be holy like him.

Reflections
from the Rust Ranch

M otoring east out of Dallas toward Arkansas and the Great Beyond on Interstate 30, alert travelers encounter an interesting roadside attraction about halfway between Greenville and Sulphur Springs. Only an hour outside the glare and concrete of the Metroplex, East Texas turns country in a hurry. Dairy farms, cotton patches, and gentlemen's ranches dot the landscape. It is obvious the freeway cut through the heart of many homesteads as cow cousins stare at intruders from positions on both sides of the blacktop.

Many of the farms look alike, a tidy brick ranch house surrounded by a variety of outbuildings, a stock tank with a decaying dock, pickup trucks in the driveway, and a smattering of implements scattered around the grounds. Pretty much what you would expect. One after another. But then, the "Rust Ranch" appears.

There is no sign hanging from the wooden arch that straddles the driveway naming this place the "Rust Ranch," but there should be. It is an amazing display of old, worn-out farm machinery lined up in symmetrical rows covering about five acres of God's turf. Included in the presentation are combines, trailers, plows, cultivators, tractors, automobiles, petroleum containers, homemade contraptions, and sundry steel objects with high rust potential.

My guess is that the machinery was brought to the location when it was about 85% worn-out, too good to take to the scrap yard (like most of the stuff in my closet), but too tired to be of any productive value. I also speculate that the caretaker had a soft spot in his heart for battle-hardened implements, and he dedicated himself to providing them a good retirement home in which to spend their graying years. I expect he positioned the stuff in rows parallel to the freeway because he expected like-minded, soft-hearted fellow farmers to stop and adopt the discarded machinery for a small administrative fee.

Now years of rain, sunshine, and neglect have transformed the lot into the "Rust Ranch." At one time, some combines were green. Others were red. A few were silver. Today, they are all classic rust. Same with the horse trailers and the tractors. The machinery comes in any color you want, as long as it is cemetery rust. (Rust isn't that bad when it is lined-up in perfectly symmetrical rows. In fact, with a little imagination, it resembles art. For my money, I like it better than the dead Cadillacs sticking out of the ground near Amarillo.)

Discarding giant steel junk in an industrial nation like ours presents a problem. If you have ever traveled the "Rustbelt" from Pittsburgh to Milwaukee, you understand something of the dilemma.

Unfortunately, steel isn't the only thing vulnerable to rust. So are people. In particular, church people.

Many churches of Jesus Christ around the country might better be described as "Rust Ranches of Christ." And nearly every church has a section of ground where rusting Christians are stationed in symmetrical rows to sit and wait for the next bout of sun and rain. It is tragic that so many disciples, regardless of age, are rusting away in church pews, useless for Kingdom farming.

Rust can be prevented. It happens when objects stop working and become stationary. Joints that are active and lubricated seldom rust shut. Machinery that is properly maintained, painted regularly, protected from harsh elements, oiled down once in awhile, and given an important task will operate indefinitely.

There is little excuse for a rusty church (see the seven churches of Asia, Revelation 2 & 3). The 21st Century will see the graying of America. Baby-boomers are going to get old, and the average age of our citizens will continue to climb. Thus, our churches are going to get older. And they have the potential to get better.

The health and spiritual success of the 21st-century church will be determined by the vitality, commitment, and industry of her senior citizens. It is imperative that our mature Christians keep their joints lubed, their hearts open, and their heads clear. God needs them to stay active in the fields.

There is the possibility that in a generation or two our churches will look like the abandoned factories of the Northern Rustbelt. To prevent such a tragedy, the church must begin today equipping its aging members for the challenges ahead. And aging disciples must respond to the call. Church sense dictates that we keep plowing fallow ground.

Don't even think about retiring! Don't purchase that rocking chair. Don't move to the lake! Don't lease that luxury liner! Don't look for ways to wind down! Don't check out! Don't fall asleep! Don't quit! Grab a can of silicone and keep those parts lubricated!

Don't Sweat the Small Stuff

Taking the family out for dinner is a great way to simplify an already complex and chaotic day. Unless your family is like ours.

We don't go out for dinner much because we can seldom agree where to go. I understand that there are freak families in which one member suggests a local restaurant and everyone else agrees, but it ain't so with our clan.

Mom likes lean grilled fish and steamed vegetables. Dad thinks *that* stuff is what you eat while the real food is frying. Boy number one won't eat anything originating in a foreign land. Boy number two doesn't like tomatoes, mushrooms, onions, lettuce, or beans. And chicken fried steak has to be served with gravy on the side. Plus we can't go to a place without free refills and hot cobbler. If it were not for the fact that we would rather compromise than starve, we might never leave the house.

The variety of options magnifies the problem. The many choices promote confusion and sponsor division. Our inherent differences of opinions, which in many circumstances prove beneficial, in this case become obstacles and points of contention. We often end up bickering over things that really don't matter while our stomachs growl in neglect.

It is frustrating because there is no clear right or wrong decision—just preferences. Mexican, Chinese, Italian, and Cajun cuisine are all good, and good people with good motives from good homes with good yards differ on which is better on Thursday evenings. Happy family meals are ones in which everyone chooses to agree on the entree.

Doing dinner and doing church have a lot of similarities.

How do good Christian brethren with a wide variety of opinions, backgrounds, experiences, and dreams stay in positive fellowship with one another when constantly confronted with a litany of viable choices? This question has never been more relevant. The personality of the 21st-century church will be largely determined by our answer.

Though not an exhaustive treatise on Christian liberty and fellowship, the 14th chapter of Romans proposes a series of inspired principles that will guide us through this complex issue (and serendipitously help us with the dinner routine).

The key principle is found in verse 15. Christ died for all people, and thus everyone is gifted with innate dignity. Your brothers and sisters command respect because Jesus gave his life for them. They must be treated like fellow heirs of salvation. They, too, are first-class folks as a result of God's mercy, and it is incumbent upon every born-again believer to love their fellow saint—no matter how different they may be. Sharing in God's love is greater than any point of division. Let all things be done in love. Live for Jesus (vss. 9, 10)!

Secondly, we must cultivate an attitude of acceptance (vs. 1) that is slow to judge and quick to accommodate. We must not look down our noses at brethren because they look, act, or think differently than we do (vs. 3). Who do we think we are, judging other servants of Jesus Christ (vs. 4)? God made us different on purpose (see Chapter 12) and it is no accident that we have different ideas, preferences, and opinions. If God counts differences as a blessing, so should we! It makes good church sense.

Thirdly, we must keep in mind that many things are not inherently right or wrong, and because they are neutral, we must remain neutral (vs. 5). French pastries, contrary to the opinion of my in-house health food freak, are not sinful. What gives one believer the right to enforce his opinion in a matter that is inconsequential? To do so invites bickering and division. Don't sweat the small stuff. There are enough issues regarding saving faith that we must not get bogged down playing trivial pursuit (vs. 17).

Lastly, we must look out for the spiritual welfare of others and spend our energies building up fellow citizens of the kingdom (vss. 18-21). At the top of our lists should be a commitment to pursue peace. **My church experience suggests that there are a handful of folks in the mix who really dig controversy and promote spiritual warfare over spiritual welfare, who would rather tear down than build up,** who would rather pick at the sore than apply salve, who prefer bickering to resolution, who would rather clutter the floor with obstacles than pick up the mess. These folks are out of line and violate the spirit of the Spirit of Peace.

Remember that the personality of the 21st-century church will be an accumulation of all our individual personalities. Does yours need some work?

Do We Shoot Trespassers?

A little crass but to the point, the bumper sticker on the back of my friend's pickup truck echoed the sentiments of his neighbors: "Don't Californicate Idaho."

For the few thousand hearty souls occupying the rugged but beautiful country of northern Idaho, Californians are the enemy. While the rest of America has worried about the Red Army and the Jamaican bobsled team for the last fifty years, folks in Idaho have battled the Californians. Their goal is simple: keep the crazy Californians out of their little world.

While many states employ big dollar public relations firms to lure immigrants from other states, native Idahonians fight to keep prospective settlers out. It is not uncommon to see Idaho promote itself as the "Beaver Fever," "Tick Fever," or "Lyme Disease" State. Locals are quick to tell visitors about rabid skunks, rampaging elk, blood-thirsty cougars, and hungry bears. Stuffed mosquitoes the size of blackbirds are mounted on walls behind cafe cash registers. Veteran tour guides are eager to show off potholes the size of Lake Michigan and mountain slides only a touch smaller than New Hampshire. They brag about eight-month winters and two-week summers. Makes for robust duck lice.

"We shoot trespassers" signs are nailed on nearly every gate. Large wolf-like dogs are stationed nearby. Vacationers are encouraged to bring their own penicillin. There is no skateboarding. Bleached hair and earrings on young men are strongly discouraged. There are no openings on local school boards or city councils. No one gives a flip how they do it in California.

Idaho, especially the lumberjacks and pioneers up north, is simply not very user-friendly regarding their coastal kissin' cousins. They don't need Californians. They don't want Californians. They don't particularly like Californians—especially in their backyard.

Idaho has an attitude. When it surpassed the million member mark a few years ago, there was wholesale dismay. They don't want to grow. If they wanted more people, crowds, and traffic, they would move to California. Most of the folks who live in North Idaho live there because you don't (truth be known, they probably think less of Texans than Californians).

How long can Idaho resist population growth and economic expansion? How long can their borders be sealed? What happens if California abandons Proposition 187, creates Proposition 188, and starts shipping its illegal immigrants to Idaho? What happens when the Gem State gets discovered? What happens if a majority of Idahonians get a new attitude?

In reviewing the isolationist tactics of these blissful wilderness people, it occurred to me that they share many similarities with church folks in heavily populated urban and suburban centers.

In many ways, churches often treat their neighbors like blue-blood Idahonians treat California trespassers. We do everything possible to keep the pagans out. We feel like we don't need the pagans. We don't want the pagans. We don't even particularly like the pagans. In fact, if we could, we wouldn't be opposed to sending them into exile, somewhere deep in Orange County.

The church has developed an unhealthy attitude toward the pagan state. Like Israel of old, we would rather ignore them than win them. We believe it is good business to discourage visitation. We turn off the lights when we see them coming up the driveway. We unleash the guard dogs and blast a few rounds of buckshot into the darkness.

We are afraid of the pagans, if for no other reason, because there are so many of them. And rather than deal with them on a regular basis, which can develop into a real hassle, we tend to believe it is better and easier to lock them out of our lives. The Barbarians are at the gate so we build bigger fences, wishing we had a wall like the ancient Chinese.

It is amazing the things we do to discourage pagans from immigrating into the church. We extend a great deal of energy sealing the Kingdom's borders. It is crazy. We are the ones who are crazy.

Let us not forget that we are called by God to be a light unto the nations, a beacon of hope to the struggling pagan, a source of life to a world operating under the dark cloud of death. Rather than remove ourselves from the darkened world, we are to engage it with the light of gospel truth. The church is a city set on a hill whose light shines brightly for all to see. The church calls its neighbors to high ground, to peace and safety in God. "Come one, come all!"

The church needs to roll out the red carpet. We need to hang welcome banners. **We need to simplify the citizenship process.** We need to become pagan-friendly. We need the attitude of Jesus who called the weary and the hassled to find rest in him (Matthew 11:28-30). We need to shoot the guard dogs and fill in the potholes.

The pagans are not our enemies. We are not in a cold war. We need to thaw the tensions with a proactive display of love. We need the pagans. We need them saved. We need them bringing their friends and family into the kingdom. We need their witness. Church sense sees value in loving the enemy.

What is your attitude toward your lost neighbors?

Easter Screams Life!

nd the angel answered and said to the women, "Do not be afraid; for I know that you are looking for Jesus who has been crucified. He is not here, for He has risen, just as He said. Come, see the place where He was lying. And go quickly and tell His disciples that He has risen from the dead; and behold, He is going before you into Galilee, there you will see Him; behold, I have told you." And they departed quickly from the tomb with fear and great joy and ran to report it to His disciples (Matthew 28:5-8).

Sunrise Service.

Easter Morning.

It is cool. And damp. A typical spring morning, except the dawn's first light is a little sharper and the mist a little heavier.

The earth's blood pressure registers higher than normal. Probably a result of bringing everything to bloom level. Winter's feeble attempt at death is foiled again. The mockingbird sings his song of life. The hills of green shout "Amen!" Life is back. Spring has sprung.

A handful of folks have gathered to celebrate the morning and contemplate their role in spring's drama. Some have come of their own free will. Others were dragged out of bed, force fed caffeine, and manually positioned among the pilgrims. And they all have emotions about the moment.

Some feel awe. Some feel awful. Some feel warm and fuzzy. Others feel hungry. Some feel like they are part of something bigger. Some feel like they would have profited more by staying in bed. Some feel liberated. Others feel manipulated. Some sense victory while the folks next door suspect it's a trick. Some feel mystery. Some feel magic. Some feel stupid. Some are flooded with emotion. Others choose a course toward oblivion.

Considering we all share the same basic blueprint, it is interesting – if not a touch odd – that we respond to cosmic history and human experience with such varied emotions.

No event packs the same emotional wallop as Easter morning. The claims engendered by the first Easter morning—that a man claiming to be the Son of God was resurrected from the dead!—strike at the heart of our emotional control centers. If it is true, then really nothing else matters. If it is false, and we've been duped, then we are people most to be pitied. This life and death stuff demands attention. Easter reminds us to number our days wisely (Psalm 90:12). It summons an emotional response. Christ's resurrection refuses to be ignored.

For believers who respond positively to Scripture's account of the empty tomb, we personally feel the gamut of emotions the first disciples experienced. In Matthew 28:8 history records that those first wide-eyed witnesses ran from the scene of the resurrection with hearts and minds full of *fear and great joy*. Emotions traditionally postured 180 degrees from one another were merged when the reality of the angel's words were processed: "He is not here, for He has risen!"

FEAR. GREAT JOY. One morning a year they are not mutually exclusive.

There is something about greatness that fosters fear. When we encounter something bigger and grander and nobler and mightier than ourselves, we usually respond with a measure of reverent fear. Ever been to the Grand Canyon or Niagara Falls? Ever seen the Northern Lights? Ever been in the path of a raging forest fire? Ever messed with a grizzly? Ever climbed aboard Shamu? Ever met God in the middle of the night on his terms? Tremble City.

Fear-sponsored reverence is a healthy thing. It brings one into a proper perspective; helps us recognize that God is God and we are not. God rolled away the stone and raised Jesus from the dead. He is the author and sustainer of life, Our Father Who Art In Heaven, the Judge of all the earth to whom we are accountable. When He acts, we ought to tremble.

Tremble with fear. Tremble with great joy. The Almighty acts —on our behalf! He did for us on the first Easter morning what we could not do for ourselves. He whipped the devil. He overcame death. He gave us the victory. He set us free. He saved our souls.

The empty tomb is a constant reminder of God's love and the source of our great, abiding joy. Easter screams life! The promise of eternal life, secured for us in the resurrection of Jesus Christ from the dead, produces unmeasured joy that sustains us through the doldrums of every common morning. It makes sense of the absurd. Great joy comes only from our great God. When you have great joy, every other emotion takes its proper place.

Easter morning prevails every morning. Can you feel it? Will you feel it?

As Good As It Gets

These are the good old days! These are the good times! This is as good as it gets!

We are living in the midst of the greatest economic boom in the history of the world. No nation has ever possessed the buying power that we presently enjoy. Never has so much money been made, spent, shuffled, borrowed, or grafted. For crying out loud, we have a tax surplus!

Look around at the construction. Look around at the consumption. Look around at the confidence. Look around at the economic concupiscence. It's here! It's there! It's everywhere! It's in the air!

We are rich!

And, yet, while it is the best of times, it is also the worst of times. A recent article in *USA Today* reports that Americans are deeper in debt than ever. We came. We saw. We charged. We continue to spend more than we make. We continue to move closer to the ragged edge of personal and national financial collapse. Bankruptcies are at record levels. Rumors persist that the reason for continued low interest rates is that if credit card companies raised their interest rates significantly, there would be so many defaults it would crush our booming economy. The distance between the "haves" and the "have-nots" grows wider and threatens the fiber of our social structure. Millions look around and ask, "Where's the wealth?" Millions more, in a futile effort to keep up with the Joneses, have mortgaged their future for a piece of today's pie. Millions more have simply given up.

We have become a nation that worships at the throne of materialism. We are more concerned with our stuff than our soul. We measure life by things rather than spiritual development. We are in a word: hedonists. We have been sold a bill of goods and the premiums are breaking us poor Americans.

I suggest that our big cars, our big houses, our big hair, and our big debt are causing us big problems.

We have been duped into believing that life consists of mere stuff and more stuff. Stupid us. Can there be any doubt "that the god of this world has blinded the minds of the unbelieving" (2 Corinthians 4:4)? Remember that our ancient adversary is not only the "father of lies," but appears "as an angel of light" to persuade us that the pursuit of wealth is always a good thing (John 8:44; 2 Corinthians 11:14). The Bible encourages us to be alert to the destructive ways of the devil: "Be alert in order that no advantage be taken of us by Satan; for we must not be ignorant of his schemes" (2 Corinthians 2:11).

Jesus says: "Beware, and be on your guard against every form of greed; for not even when one has an abundance does his life consist of his possessions" (Luke 12:15).

Jesus doesn't say this to throw cold water on your economic pursuits. He's not attempting to deprive you of investment opportunities. Jesus is not advocating that you host a garage sale and join the ranks of those on welfare.

In fact, Jesus is more concerned about your overall welfare than you are. What He is promoting is a balanced life. We often forget that we are body and soul, and both need nurturing. Jesus reminds us that if we spend all our energies pursuing material things, then spiritual bankruptcy is inevitable. "What is a man profited if he gains the whole world and loses his soul" (Matthew 16:26, KJV)?

Money is not inherently evil. Remember that it is "the love of money [that] is the root of all evil" (1 Timothy 6:10, KJV). It is a matter of priorities. Jesus gently reminds us: "where your treasure is, there will your heart be also" (Luke 12:34). What concerns the Lord is our possession obsession. It is the obsession that is the problem. Instead, he tells us to "seek first His kingdom and His righteousness, and everything we need will be given to us" (Matthew 6:33).

Is your garage full but your heart empty? Do your charge cards no longer give you an adrenaline buzz? Are you paying more taxes but enjoying it less? Have you found the road to riches to be a dangerous highway? Would you like to trade all your stuff for lasting contentment? Do you want real freedom? Are you interested in making sense of the boom? Then Jesus has a deal for you!

The truth is that the pursuit of financial freedom is usually the road to bondage. We become slaves to our stuff, and the god of this world is a cruel taskmaster. Jesus offers real liberation from debt. He gives us truth, "and the truth will set us free!" (John 8:32).

It is folly to trust in riches (Psalm 29). It is wise to trust in God (Psalm 34). Remember that the Y3K disaster is just around the bend.

Are You All Right?

Three of the finest Christian men I know are also longtime quail hunting buddies. These brothers are of the serious ilk. They have lots of hyper, smelly dogs, fowl leases all over west Texas, and buy their bird food by the silo! From October through February they conduct most of their mission activities under the starry Texas skies of the beautiful I-20 corridor between Ranger and Sweetwater.

To justify their excesses, they often coerce unsuspecting alpha-male wannabes into joining their weekend adventures. Few return to the safety of their Metroplex dwellings in better shape than they left. Few can handle this much fun.

One weekend last fall they took a brother who was an experienced hunter, but a rookie adventurist. They hit the road early on a Friday morning and were marching through the dead grass south of Abilene by noon. As they tell it, birds were everywhere and by dusk they had their bags full and were back at camp for dinner. Dinner, I am told, was comprised of juicy beef ribs and fried potatoes. I have often wondered why they go quail hunting and eat beef, but if one were to begin pointing out such inconsistencies, it would be a long spell before one could find a tidy finishing point.

Anyway, as the story goes, their visitor started laughing at one of their wild stories and choked on a mouthful of gristle. As his face turned blue, the other three guys turned his way and expressed concern. "Are you all right?" they asked. He shook his head side to side. They repeated the question and this time he responded by hacking up some meat. For these fellows, staying calm was not a problem. "Are you all right now?" they asked again. And again he shook his head "no." No reason to get excited. He had a good breath about thirty seconds prior to the event, so nothing real bad should happen for another thirty. One more time they approached the subject from the comfort of their lawn chairs. "Do you think you are going to be all right?" As he fell over and bounced off the rented earth, he coughed up a huge chunk of deceased cow and gasped for air. They kindly assisted him back to his assigned position at the campfire and got back to the important business of relaxing in the country.

My friend laughs at the situation now, but did say they were all a little concerned at the time.

It occurred to me that we church folks often treat the unchurched like a bunch of seasoned quail hunters breaking in a rookie outdoor enthusiast.

The unchurched are turning blue in the face, choking on the gristle of sin, and we simply smile at them from the comfort of our lawn chairs and ask if they think they are going to be okay. We don't rush to their aid and slam them on the back or perform a primitive Heimlich move or squeeze the gristle out of them. We don't get excited about their plight. We casually muse over their need for a breath of fresh air, but we are more concerned with our own oxygen intake. We pray that when they fall out of the chair, they will bounce hard enough to dislodge the obstruction and return to the campfire circle. Church sense dictates that we probably ought to be more concerned.

A Sense of Expectation

O f all the special interest groups, I like expectant mothers best. I like the color of their cheeks. I like the way they walk. I like their intensity. Expectant mothers have heightened senses. They are more aware of life than the rest of us.

There is something about living with a sense of expectation that brings vibrancy to the daily journey. Have you ever shared a domicile with a five-year-old who is having a big birthday party on Saturday? They are wired with energy. Don't you love working with someone who is leaving for a two-week cruise on Friday? It is an understatement to say they lack focus. Remember graduation day? Your wedding day? Your first car? Your first house? Your first shock treatment? Your first hayride? Your first kiss?

It seems that everyone who looks forward with hopeful expectation has an extra spring in their step. **Looking forward to tomorrow instead of worrying about tomorrow brings a whole different perspective to the daily grind.** We can endure much hardship and nearly any obstacle if we are energized by the promise of a better tomorrow. Call it hope.

Disciples of hope measure their journey by a different standard than do the pleasure-mongers. Their basis for happiness and contentment is established in the confident expectation of a secure future. Expectant mothers waddle through nine months of physical discomfort because they know the fruit of their labor will produce a new life. College kids stay up late and study hard because they want to graduate in May, get a good job, and reimburse their parents. Worker bees suffer the indignities of the nine-to-five insanity because next month they are headed to the beach for two weeks of fun and sun. **An expectant hope for tomorrow fuels our todays.**

Nowhere is the sense of expectancy more intense than in the church of Jesus Christ. Ever since Jesus departed this earth, the church has lived with the promise of His imminent return. Perhaps today! Perhaps tomorrow! Perhaps next week!

Of all the special interest groups and of all the special future events, Christians and the return of their Savior Jesus Christ are the brightest. The church of Christ has a lot of things going for it, but none as good as its future—a future founded on the promise of a God Who cannot lie!

It saddens me that not every believer is motivated and energized by this acute sense of expectation. Many folks are cheating themselves out of the fullness of the Christian experience by forfeiting the joy promised in a better forever. What about you? What floats your boat? If it is anything but the return of Jesus and the hope of eternal life, then you are on the wrong channel.

I saw a bumper sticker recently that said: "Jesus is coming. Look busy." I laughed. I cried. I made my own bumper sticker. It says: "Jesus is coming. Rejoice!"

We worry a lot about restoring the first-century church. We strive to duplicate their pattern, but might be better served duplicating their intensity for the *parousia*. This focus may light the fires of discipleship and evangelism. If we want to restore primitive Christianity, it must begin by restoring the passion they felt for the return of the Lord (1 Thessalonians 1; 2 Peter 3; James 5; John 14; 1 Corinthians 1)! We can get the stuff right, but if we don't get the promise right, we fail miserably (and often live miserably). True church sense must be filtered through future sense.

Don't let millennial wackos and their wild apocalyptic predictions leave you with a bitter taste about the Lord's return. Ignore the dodo birds who think they can manipulate or figure out the date of Christ's return. Instead simply cling to the promise that when the time is right, He will be back! It may be today! Maranatha! His promises are true! The future is ours!

Half Dead

For to me, to live is Christ, and to die is gain. But if I am to live on in the flesh, this will mean fruitful labor for me; and I do not know which to choose. But I am hard-pressed from both directions, having the desire to depart and be with Christ, for that is very much better, yet to remain on in the flesh is more necessary for your sake (Paul in Philippians, Chapter 1).

The Apostle Paul was an amazing fellow for many reasons. Among them was his perspective about life and death. There seemed to be little doubt in his mind that this temporary stay on planet Earth is nothing more than a short prelude to eternal life. His longing to depart this life and take up heavenly residence permeates much of his writing. He believed that Jesus had a mansion waiting for him on Jordan's yonder shore, and he desired to fill the reservation ASAP. He lived in the present, but his heart and soul were in the eternal future.

We can fairly conclude that Paul knew what it is to be half dead. In similar fashion, it would enhance our pilgrimage if we developed a healthy view of what it is to be alive in Christ and dead to the world. We need to understand that like Paul, we too, are half dead.

Perhaps an illustration will help us recognize our true condition.

My nephew Beau celebrated his sixth birthday with a big party at a local hotel. My sister hosted the party at a neutral sight, not only to protect her private property from the destructive nature of her son's running buddies, but because the Inn granted access to the swimming pool. My sister is always thinking creatively—and defensively.

Before the presents and after the cake, my nephew and one of his pals left the main group of splashers and ventured into the adjoining kiddy pool. There he discovered under the surface a steel drain cover separating the two pools. For fifteen years the cover had been at peace, undisturbed by legions of visiting children. It looked too comfortable for Beau, so he submerged himself and ripped the cover from the pool wall to further investigate its role in the cosmic order of things.

This action created a reaction with Beau caught in the real action. The pressure difference between the two pools generated a weird sort of "Twenty Thousand Leagues Under the Sea" vacuum that sucked Beau's six year old head into the drain.

My sister was alerted to the problem when his swimming partner jumped out of the pool and started screaming, "Beau's head is stuck in the sewer!" My sister sprinted to the scene, jumped in the pool, grabbed her son by the waist and pulled. And jerked. And yanked. And wrenched. And he didn't budge. He was stuck. Stuck real good. The big pool wanted him. The little pool had him. And they were having a serious tug-of-war over who would end up with him.

By something more than luck, his head turned a little, the seal broke, and the deep surrendered its captive. The Jonah experience was concluded.

After a few moments of coughing, spitting, and shaking, the blue left his cheeks, and he once again became an oxygen sponsored mammal—much to the delight of his mother and peers. It could have been a tragic end to a great party.

The event left a dramatic impression on Beau Bomber. He has slowed down, at times to a normal pace. He is more cautious. He is quick to stop, look, and listen. He doesn't enter the pool until an hour after he has eaten. He doesn't play with snakes, sharp objects, or the criminally insane. He has developed a keen sense of value for the sanctity of human life—especially his own.

Recently Beau stayed with my folks at their mountain home. A few moments before the sun settled in for the night, the local coyote population burst into song and scared the bejeepers out of Beau. He sprinted for the house, locked the door behind him, and jumped on Grandma's lap. Trying to comfort the boy, the big people explained the harmless nature of Wiley Coyote. Beau didn't buy it. Finally when pressed why he wouldn't go back outside, he responded, "I know what it is to be half dead!"

Do you?

Before the Warranty Expires

H appiness is. . . having something break while still under warranty!

Seldom does it happen. Most devices are manufactured to self-destruct a few months after the warranty expires. Once in a great while the covert agents of industry foul up and a product blows its top or bottom while still the responsibility of the creator. When it happens, we consumers are ecstatic—and a little bit cocky.

Our new house was fifty weeks old when I finally conducted an all out effort to get the warranty related defects repaired. The furnace folks rehung some pipe. Electricians restrung some wire. Carpet men stretched. Roofers reshuffled. Painters stroked. And the general contractor crossed off the days on his calendar.

The last item on my checklist was the sprinkler system. It was last because I was too embarrassed to tell the installer that I'm not smart enough to operate the timer. Finally, out of necessity, I humbled myself and called him. Turned out the timer and I weren't the problems. I had the sprinklers operating properly. Unfortunately, all the water was running under my driveway and cascading to the surface between seams in the concrete and sending a small river down the alley toward Ten Mile Creek.

Not to worry. It was under warranty. I did not mean for it to happen, but somehow all these warranty claims at one time made me smug. Call it leverage, something to which I'm so unaccustomed that I proved to be unable to handle it. Having the upper hand can be a formula for failure.

I called the sprinkler guy. Told him there was a problem with *his* equipment. And *his* installation. And *his* truck and trailer. And *his* profession. Told him he had better hustle out and take care of *his* problem. He didn't want an unhappy homeowner like me on his tail. No, sir!

He came. He smiled. He said he would have it fixed in an hour, no charge. I told him that is what I expected, since I had the warranty and the leverage. "Take heed when you stand, lest you fall," a little voice whispered.

I wasn't really rude, just smug and senseless. I'm not really that way. Power had temporarily corrupted me.

An hour later, the contractor knocked on the back door. When I answered it, the big galoot was on the porch sponsoring a suspiciously smug smile. "Can you come here a moment, Mr. Carlson?" He moved toward the scene of the accident with more confidence than an hour ago.

"Look here," he said, pointing to a freshly dug hole next to the driveway. "It appears that one of your sprinkler heads is broken."

"Yea," I said under my breath, "probably faulty equipment or installation."

"It's not only broken, Mr. Carlson, it's crushed. Probably been run over by a big truck." He then looked away from me and stared admiringly at my truck. "Probably a big, blue Ford truck."

There sat my truck, egg all over its face, plastic sprinker parts stuck in the tread of the right front tire. Stupid truck.

I managed a faint smile. He grinned from ear to ear, as if I was the seventh smug property owner he had humiliated before noon.

"Can I pay you for your time?" I begged, desperately hoping he would dispense enough grace for me to survive the day. No such luck.

"Nope," he said, "I'll give you this one."

He then sauntered to his truck, smugly rolled down the window, hung his arm out, and grinned like Davy Crockett at a bear. "Call me if I can ever be of any help."

I crawled back to the house a beaten but wiser man. Lord, have mercy on all us smug sinners.

I hope God recalls me before the warranty runs out.

1-800-IT'S GRACE

hat a shame. "Jacko" *mysteriously* disappeared somewhere between his British Columbian forest home and the novelty-starved Victorian English capitol. An 1884 newspaper story provides the account of Jacko's captors attempting to transport the hairy beast across the Atlantic. The early settlers who followed the railroad into eastern British Columbia were sure they had captured the regional bogeyman—a real live sasquatch. But, poof, he was gone. Another victim of the Bermuda Triangle? Only the legend—not the proof—remains.

Since Jacko's fifteen minutes of fame, thousands of individual reports have surfaced claiming personal encounters with the illusive creature now called Bigfoot. Sometimes it is a quick glance of a large, hairy brute disappearing into the forest. Other times it is the discovery of an unusual campsite formerly occupied by large beasts exhibiting hints of civility. Then there are the times when Bigfoot goes unseen, but not unsmelled. Firsthand witnesses insist the stench is unmistakable. Nothing stinks up a place like Bigfoot, nature's most hygienically challenged critter. Numerous folks have related tales of frightening encounters with Bigfoot where their cabins were pelted with rocks and their campsites attacked. But for the most part, Bigfoots appear to be shy creatures who shun human contact. They don't speak to the media.

Primary evidence for Bigfoot's existence is the tracks he leaves behind. A 700 pound vertical beast can make some impressive impressions. Nearly 600 sets of tracks have been collected and studied over the last forty years, and one expert, Dr. W. Flenner Farenback, steadfastly argues they are the real deal. Dr. John Napier backs him up: "The footprints are biologically convincing." Another certified anthropologist, Dr. Grover Krantz from Washington State University, has reconstructed the skeletal structure of Bigfoot's big foot, and not only is it big but unique in a manner that proves it ain't a Grizzly or a half-drunk Saturday night hoaxter.

Hoping to demonstrate that Bigfoot is something more than the human imagination's need for a creature larger than life, the Academy of Applied Science is presently financing a Bigfoot Research Project managed by 70-year-old native Irishman Peter Byrne. He cruises the forests of the Pacific Northwest during the days and returns to his cabin at night to screen over a hundred calls received on the 1-800-BIG-FOOT hotline. Sightings have increased now that folks know someone cares.

I grew up in the heart of Bigfoot Country, for awhile living up the road from Jacko's hangout. Sightings were a common occurrence around our neck of the woods. However I was raised in a family of skeptics—unbelievers who blamed strong drink and fertile imaginations. I always hoped I would see one, but never did, not even from afar. (I did one time, though, stumble on the world's largest Lady Bug mating grounds. I've kept it to myself until now, afraid of public ridicule.)

How many sightings does it take to make something a real possibility? I ask this question not so much because I am trying to legitimize Bigfoot's existence, but because Grace sightings have been pouring into the church, and I have this growing suspicion that there might be something to it. Can this many people be wrong?

Folks of different ages, backgrounds, races, and political persuasions, many of them reputable and trustworthy folks, have reported authentic contacts with Grace. Many claim their legalistic campsites have been rudely disrupted by God's love and their sectarian cabins pelted with wet rocks from mercy's stream. What is going on? Tracks in the creek bank weren't made by human efforts.

Can it be that Grace is more than a distant rumor, more than a figment of our fecund imaginations, more than an eerie, shy creature lurking in the shadows of the dense secular forest? Oh, my! Grab the kids and run for shelter! God is on the loose!

What kind of evidence supports these radical claims? Are there actual sightings, tracks, smells, videos, life changes, heart changes, attitude changes?

Consider what people are saying on the 1-800-IT'S-GRACE hotline:

☛ **Forgiveness.** What more proof do you need? Folks are receiving and dispensing forgiveness in supernatural doses. One victim reports being overwhelmed by God's forgiveness, knocked to the floor by the realization that God worked in Jesus to forgive *all* her sins. The story goes that Jesus Christ has brought "redemption through His blood, the forgiveness of our trespasses, according to the riches of His grace, which He lavished upon us" (Ephesians 1:6-8). Wow! Can you believe that? Another man reports that a brother forgave him of an ugly act for no other motive than Scripture's injunction to "be kind, tenderhearted to one another, forgiving others as God in Christ also forgave you" (Ephesians 4:32).

I had a brother disclose recently that he forgave his parents for their dysfunctional ways. They didn't even ask for it. He did it anyway. It is driving them crazy. They think he is on drugs. Nope. Better. He's on love! What next? People forgiving their kids? Their spouses? Their siblings? Where will it end? Earth forbid!

☛ **Confidence.** There is really no other explanation for eternal confidence than grace. "Let us therefore draw near with confidence to the throne of grace, that we may receive mercy and may find grace to help in time of need" (Hebrews 4:16). Sightings are increasing in frequency and intensity. Whole families report that they have turned their souls and their eternities over to God. They have been heard to say that they trust him; that he is able to finish what he started; that because he is faithful, we can have confidence in the day of judgement (1 John 4:17). Mind boggling! What if it is true? What if we have to depend on God? What if it is more than an urban myth! Quick, someone stomp this out before it spreads!

But rumors persist. One ancient editorial suggests that God wants us saved more than we do, and He is both willing and able to make it happen. Well, what happens if we believe in grace? Where does it leave us? Confident. Assured. Relaxed. Hopeful. Joyous. Blessed. Maybe we ought to pay more attention to the whispers and the rumbles. "Our God, through the Lord Jesus Christ, has loved us and given us eternal comfort and good hope by grace" (2 Thessalonians 2:16).

☛ **Changed lives.** The clearest evidence available that Grace has emerged from the dark and foreboding forest is witnessed in the changed lives of true believers. "Grace is instructing us to deny ungodliness and worldly desires, and to live sensibly, righteously, and godly in the present age, looking for the blessed hope and the appearing of the glory of our great God and Savior, Christ Jesus" (Titus 2:11-14).

I've seen it myself. Even though I didn't grow up in Grace country, I know it when I see it. I have hard proof in the tracks it leaves behind. There are footprints of love, peace, and ministry everywhere.

Got to go. I just saw something move in the woods.

Coloring outside the Lines

T he menacing presence of baseball's most recent pitching phenomenon recently occupied the front cover of *Sports Illustrated* magazine. Pedro Martinez, the new "Dominican Dandy," is cocked and ready to deliver high, hard heat under a caption that reads: "He's so good, it's scary."

The young fireballer is this generation's answer to yesterday's legends. He brings to mind the likes of past heroes from Walter Johnson to Nolan Ryan. And he is good. Folks who pay attention to these matters say he is very good. His fastball flirts with radar guns as it approaches triple figures. His change-up, like Nolan's, buckles the knees of unsuspecting hitters. He also throws a variety of weird stuff, baffling opponents and teammates alike. A nasty rumor is afloat that he sometimes throws at the batter rather than the catcher. In a word: intimidating.

Yet, something is wrong with this pitcher. Pedro is a normal size guy. Unlike the prototypical behemoth with a glandular problem, the young righthander has the physical construction of a bat boy.

Major League pitchers are supposed to be big—like 6'3" and 220 pounds. Most *Big* League pitching staffs look like an accumulation of NFL linebackers. The theory is that the bigger the man, the harder he throws.

Not so with Pedro. He defies baseball sense.

"By conventional standards Martinez is a freak. He is listed at 5'11" and 170 pounds, but appears even smaller in person. He has scant muscle definition, and his long, soft face makes him look about as intimidating as a mall cop." The Sports Illustrated article goes on to say, "When his unimposing appearance is mentioned, Martinez smiles and says, 'Why don't you grab a bat, then we'll see.'"

No thanks.

Pedro has had to overcome many obstacles in his climb to stardom, but none greater than the preconceived standards of the establishment. Odds were against him. He didn't fit the mold. He wasn't the right shape. He didn't meet the established qualifications.

Over the course of time and for a variety of reasons, organizations, institutions, corporations, civilizations, and leagues develop a destructive tendency to crystallize their images of how things and people should appear. Oftentimes, these stereotypical definitions become detrimental to body life. Generalizations and preferences somehow evolve into code, and once a code is established and signed into law, it is stuffed full of preservatives and guaranteed a long shelf life. Few know how or where the Law of the Medes and the Persians was constructed, but changing it requires constitutional revision and a two-thirds majority.

One of our most serious human flaws is the predisposition to favor the established and to discount the exceptional. In so doing, we often become our own worst enemy. Instead, we must mature to the point that biases and prejudices no longer cripple our growth as a civilization or an organization. Hold to that which warrants allegiance, but surrender whatever is detrimental to the mission. Look for new possibilities. Embrace growth. Consider the exceptional.

Sam Walton wasn't Ivy League schooled, but he made a pretty good CEO. Abe Lincoln was a country hick from the Western Frontier, but history ranks him as our best president. "If God wanted man to fly, he would have given him wings." The Wright brothers were dreamers. Their ideas were for the birds. "You can't let women vote; next thing you know, they will be running the world."

And they were right. "David can't be king. He is only an insignifi-
cant little shepherd boy—obviously not Big League material."

If there is one story from history that should make us cautious about judging by external appearances, it is the biblical
account of God anointing Jesse's youngest son as a future Hall-
of-Famer.

The amazing story of David's unlikely ascent to the throne
begins in 1 Samuel 16. It is here we encounter the grizzled
prophet Samuel trudging along the rocky path to Jesse's farm in
hope of securing Israel's next ruler. Saul, at one time Israel's
favorite son, had fallen into serious disfavor with God because of
his stubborn and rebellious heart, and sometime before breakfast
Samuel had ripped the kingdom from his possession. A replace-
ment had been selected by God, and Samuel was led to Jesse's
place for a sneak preview of next year's model king.

Jesse received the prophet and proceeded to march his seven
sons before him. All were royal material, but all were rejected by
God. Seven was not enough. Out of frustration more than pomp,
Samuel inquired of Jesse, "Are these all the children?" Dad hesi-
tated. "There remains yet the youngest, and behold, he is tending the sheep." In other words, "I have a boy, but surely you are
not serious about examining him." Samuel cocked his head in
prophetic fashion, looked coldly at the once proud father, and
threw Jesse a high, hard one: "Bring him here, because no one
sits down until I see him."

Jesse was embarrassed about the whole deal. He had already
provided his best stock for inspection; they were rejected, and he
thought the prophet wanted to rub a little salt in his wounded
ego. Under compulsion he fetched boy number eight from the
field and offered him to God. Apologetically, he tried to explain
the boy's soft features and ruddy complexion. He was sorry he
was handsome. Samuel looked once, looked twice. Looked three
times, and thought to himself, "God can't be serious!" Now
Samuel was embarrassed.

Humans are too easily embarrassed.

God presented and endorsed the lowly shepherd boy, nudged
Samuel and said, "Arise, anoint him, for this is he."

Jaws dropped. Minds raced. Hearts fluttered.

Samuel gathered his thoughts, gathered the incredulous siblings together, and removed the sacred horn of oil from his breast pocket. He popped the top and slowly poured it on David's head. As it ran down his boyish face and dripped from his chin onto his clothes, the stunned spectators tried to process the meaning of the moment. While they pondered, the Spirit of the Lord came mightily upon David.

And the Lord said to Samuel, "Do not look at his appearance or at the height of his stature . . . for God sees not as man sees, for man looks at the outward appearance, but the Lord looks at the heart."

If the decision had been left to Samuel and Jesse, Eliab would have been king. He was tall and handsome like Saul. The royal photographers and media representatives would have loved him. He looked the part. He fit the mold. He met the established requirements of the establishment.

But God does not see as man sees.

Centuries later, David's son came to Jerusalem to receive the Kingdom prophesied to the Shepherd-King (2 Samuel 7:12-16). But he did not look the part. He was from Galilee. His dad was a carpenter. He inherited an unacceptable pedigree. His education was suspect. He hung around with common folks. He messed with the Sabbath. Rumors of scandal surrounded his birth. He had no stately form or majesty nor appearance that would attract people. He favored those on the outside and challenged those on the inside. He rode a donkey and not a stallion. He violated every criteria in the Messiah Manual. He did not look good in the team uniform. He did not fit the mold. He did not act like a savior.

Thus he was despised and forsaken of men. He was oppressed, and he was afflicted. He was rejected, and he was executed. And he found favor with the Father.

He was God's chosen Son, sent by the Father to reconcile the world. "He came to his own, but his own received him not" (John 1:11, KJV). Rejected by man; glorified by God. Jesus couldn't meet human expectations, yet his sinless life qualified him to serve as the perfect sacrifice. He alone, saved the world—including you!

Many lessons can be learned from Pedro, David, and Jesus Christ. Sectarian thinkers must be reminded not to make rules where rules are not required. There is grave danger in building boxes for prescribed behavior and predetermined limits. Minor League thinking stunts development. Sometimes God colors outside the lines. We must all be careful how we evaluate our world and our Christian fellowship. Sometimes church sense contradicts common sense. We should heed the reminder of Scripture that sometimes we are dealing with an angel when our earthly receptors only see a bum. We would be wise to evaluate others by the same standard God employs—what is in the heart? Black to us can be white to God. White to us can be black to God. Don't be deceived by appearances. Seek a mature wisdom that can look past the surface to the heart of the matter and the person. See as God sees.

Thank God that he does not judge us by outward appearance only. None of us are prototypical saints. None of us match up. And thank God that he does not see us as prototypical sinners without an opportunity for eternal life. God looks beyond our Minor League performance to our Big League potential.

Cold War Nonsense

A number of social pundits suggest that America is worse off since the end of the Cold War. They contend that our icy conflict with the Soviet Union sponsored a healthy economy and a sense of purpose that is currently lacking. What this country needs is not another five-cent cigar, but a new evil empire on which we can focus our hostilities. What fun is life if you don't have someone with whom to fight? Who are we going to blame for our troubles? What new distraction can we manufacture?

Not to worry!

The original Cold War is alive and well—or more appropriately—not so well! Long before the U.S. and the U.S.S.R. decided that tension and conflict would highlight their relationship, mankind and God have been at odds. And perhaps the best way to describe this on-again/off-again dispute is in terms of a cold war. Seldom are there open hostilities; instead the two sides simply don't get along. It is senseless posturing on our part.

The skirmish between the two superpowers following WWII was based on their mutual desire for ultimate power. Same thing goes for God and mankind. God has all the power, and we want it, and we won't be satisfied until we dethrone God. He is the supernatural power, and although we are nothing but pitiful wannabes, it is still great fodder for conflict. In this cold war only one side is at fault. We are the ones who don't make sense.

Why are we engaged in a cold war we can't win? Why is there so much tension between God and us? Simple. God is holy. We are profane and common. God is righteous. We stink. God has it. We want it. He is in charge. We hate authority. God holds us accountable. We don't like it. All the components are in place for a nasty little war.

Is this the crazy kind of destructive relationship that you have chosen? If it is, I suggest you surrender, sign a treaty, and throw yourself at the mercy of the Great Sovereign. God doesn't want a war. Tension and conflict exist because we sinners perpetuate the hostilities by living in sin and rebellion. The cold war with God is our doing, and it is a battle we can't win. The sooner relations are normalized, the better off we will be. God signed the peace treaty with Christ's blood. Now he hands the pen to you.

Church Them

I'll tell you why we need legalized abortion," she screamed, her right index finger waving violently in the air. "I work in a hospital and every day I see pregnant women who aren't fit to be mothers!"

As the blood drained from her face and her finger resumed a more orthodox position, I considered igniting another tirade, but decided it was best to fashion a silent rebuttal. Call it safe sex talk.

There are a number of questions that deserve a response in regard to her contemporary line of reasoning, but the glaring issue is *who* determines who is fit and who ain't?

Herein lies the problem with the secular mind. A thought process devoid of biblical principles embraces raw pragmatism. It is worldly sense at its brutal worst. In our postmodern culture many folks see the world without an objective standard for what constitutes right and wrong. Instead, decisions are based upon what feels good to the individual and not upon a code of values delivered by a God greater than the individual. Truth becomes personal property, and the individual legislates subjective morality based on experience, appetite, and whim. The Ten Commandments become the Ten Committee Recommendations. Life begins and ends when "I" say so. Freedom of choice becomes

God, and his throne is usurped by King Self. "Do not murder" has its claws removed. Postmodern thinkers hate to get scratched.

Perhaps the deepest chasm separating those with a Christian worldview and a Bible-based ethic from those of the secular realm with an individual-based ethic is the way social issues are addressed. Christians mirror the biblical view that adultery is wrong and there are consequences to sin. Secularists position themselves to evaluate multiple sexual relationships from the standpoint of how it feels and what it accomplishes. It is law vs. pragmatism. Christian thinkers echo the biblical teaching that abortion is murder. Postmodern thinkers ridicule biblical authority and demand freedom of choice to do what they want, when they want, where they want, how they want. They become irritated and angry if there are negative consequences to their actions, frequently blaming the Christian system for their guilt. Keep in mind that the pagan mind believes freedom is found outside law. This is fundamentally different from the biblical worldview that teaches freedom can only be found in God's law. Judeo-Christian moral traditions are square pegs in postmodern circles.

Consider again the phrase, "Women who aren't fit to be mothers." Pragmatically this may true. We all know women who are terrible mothers and men who are terrible fathers. But we also know women who were bad women and *became* great mothers. We know men who were wild and crazy and turned it around to become outstanding dads. There are children who overcome great obstacles to become great adults. I'm glad Abraham Lincoln and Sammy Sosa were not aborted. The real problem with this argument is that it puts the burden of deciding who is and who isn't on the individual, and we all know how unstable individuals are prone to be.

What if 51% of the individuals convene in Cleveland one day and decide that left-handed people or tall people or white people or retarded people or northern people or girl people or Christian people are not fit to be people? Do we murder these nonpeople, too? What if this week we think nearsighted people are better off dead than lasered? What if old people become as defenseless as unborn people? What if you become as helpless as an unborn child? What if Mom wants to dispose of you because you are more work than you are worth? Princeton University's infamous ethicist Dr. Singer currently advocates Mom ought to have at least thirty days to decide if junior is a keeper. And he has a following. You nervous?

This is not a new problem. Since the beginning there has been conflict between those who practice law and those who practice pragmatism. Satan convinced Adam and Eve they would be better off without the long arm of God's law. They learned they could run but they couldn't hide. Later biblical history records the dark world of the "Judges" where "every person did what was right in the sight of their own eyes." Pretty scary, huh?

The great battle of the 21st century will be fought between the ears. What principles, what senses, what Spirit, will guide us as a culture and a republic? Forget the fact that this nation was founded and grounded in biblical law. Our constitution is being systematically undermined by pragmatic specialists in all three branches of government. **Abortion is legal and remains legal, not because it is right, but because the majority of Americans don't want to be burdened with biblical law.** Greed, graft, violence, adultery, and a litany of other sins run rampant because lots of folks in our world like doing their own thing. Obviously, mankind left to their own without respect for God's law will drift into anarchy. Postmodern man roars like a noble beast, but in reality he is a very sick and helpless creature, easy prey for the prowling devil.

How do you combat the screaming, finger-waving secularists of your world? Love them. Convert them. Church them. Our only hope is that the God of all mercy will regenerate their sin-sick hearts and set them free from the horrible bonds of self-worship. Doing our own thing must be replaced with doing God's thing. Heaven help us if postmodern man ever commandeers planet Earth, takes over the controls, and decides whose ticket is valid to ride.

Church Matters

Many social scientists believe that church (not necessarily spirituality) will become increasingly irrelevant in the 21st century. Trends indicate that lots of younger folks are suspicious of organized religion and suspect of institutional faith. They tell the pollsters that they want spirituality without formal religious affiliation. Some call it the privatization of faith. I call it a bunch of bunk.

I absolutely refuse to believe that church doesn't matter. I would have to be a fool to swallow the idea that culture is going to get so sophisticated in the 21st century that church somehow grows outdated.

Granted, there will always be religious rebels and rugged spiritual individualists. Church has never been and never will be for everybody—although it could be if everybody would give it a chance. Church has rules and some don't like rules. For folks not willing to play by God's rules, church can be a hassle. Without apology, Christ's church demands that folks love, serve, behave, and respond like the manual dictates. Unreasonable? I don't think so, but obviously others do. I pray that God will rewire their logic chip.